HIDDEN TREASURES

DORSET

Edited by Allison Dowse

First published in Great Britain in 2002 by
YOUNG WRITERS
Remus House,
Coltsfoot Drive,
Peterborough, PE2 9JX
Telephone (01733) 890066

All Rights Reserved

Copyright Contributors 2002

HB ISBN 0 75433 980 7
SB ISBN 0 75433 981 5

FOREWORD

This year, the Young Writers' Hidden Treasures competition proudly presents a showcase of the best poetic talent from over 72,000 up-and-coming writers nationwide.

Young Writers was established in 1991 and we are still successful, even in today's technologically-led world, in promoting and encouraging the reading and writing of poetry.

The thought, effort, imagination and hard work put into each poem impressed us all, and once again, the task of selecting poems was a difficult one, but nevertheless, an enjoyable experience.

We hope you are as pleased as we are with the final selection and that you and your family continue to be entertained with *Hidden Treasures Dorset* for many years to come.

CONTENTS

Alderney County Middle School

Lauren Wareham	1
Alex Buckland	1
Sammy Terrell	2
Danielle Clark	2
Jodie Lillington	3
Sophie Mudge	3
Kayleigh Collbourne	4
Kyle Stacey	4
Anastasia Day	5
Victoria Bridgeman	5
Isabelle Mitchell	6

All Saints CE Primary School

Dylan Frost	6
Cicely Clasby	7
Laurence Atchison	7
Emma Murcer	8
Andrew Read	8
Mark Capon	9
Tim Bailey	10
Hephzibah Watts	10
Sam Buckland	11
Casey Brown	12
Natasha Wiltshire	13
Jessica Winsper	14
Ben Brotherwood	14

Knighton House School

Susie Coreth	15
Memmi Rasmussen	15
India Lewis	16
Rebecca Sutton	16
Sophie Thorpe	17
Milly Donaldson	17

Emily Girkins	18
Iona Woods	18
Jenny McCavitt	19
Eliza Sketchley	19
Polly Meyer	20

Motcombe Grange School

Pippa Beard	21
Rebecca Antill	22
Georgina Alice Stopford	22
Eliza Hamer	23
Henrietta Dillon	24
Leo Dexter	24
Beatrice Herbert	25
Alice McKeith	26

St Andrew's Primary School, Weymouth

Annabel Lane	26
Victoria McNern	27
Bryony Bratchell	27
Lauren Bourne	28
Domonic Sorokopud	28
Chloe Drew	28
Jennie Martin	29
Rosie Prior	29
Victoria Browne	30
James Almond	30
Zoey Peppin	31
Chelsea Ratcliffe	31
Christopher Kitching	31
Steven Rockett	32
Madeleine Puleston	32
Danielle Green	33
Lisa Harrington	33
Rachel Sykes	34
Amelia Bull	34
Ellen Norman	35
Stuart Felstead	35

Sapphira Pratt	36
Robyn Welford	36
Cerys Jones	37
Zoë Day	37
Philip Cole	38
Warren Hicks	38
Benjamin Woodland	38
Francesca Guarraci	39
Sam Shurey	39
Jordan Emburey	40
Emma Taylor	40
Verity Witt	41
Grace Passoni	41
Amy Small	42
Barney Moss	43
Adam Wiggins	44
Stacey Mills	45
Joshua Betts	46
Thomas Barnes	47
Maxim Sorokopud	48
Melissa Mahon	49
Alice Bell	50
Aaron Sherlock	51
Stacey Green	52
Natalie Craig	53
James Cole	54
Cassie Hall	55
Katie Dawling	56
Catherine Burridge	57
Michael Whittle	58
Joseph Butcher	59
Harry McWilliams	60
Katherine Houston	61
James Davis	62
Emily Hurst	63
Kelley Ireland	64
Tamara Collier	65
Jennifer Derrett	66

Charlotte Kaiser	67
Daniel Houston	68
Jemma Tewkesbury	69
Hal Barker	70
Chloe Groves	71
George Lane	72
Maxwell Vallance	73
Tommy Jones	74
Luke Davis	75
Danielle Luke	75

St George's School, Bourton

Karl Newton	75
Naomi Samuelson	76
Harriet Walker	76
Olivia Worthington	77
Oliver Swan	77
Lottie Lobb	78
Maddy Hollick	78
Tom Barton	79
Lian Willow Denyer	79
Natalie Birley	80
Sam Bingham	80
Daniel Turner	81
Jake McClung	82
Tasmin Hunt	82
Garreth Ball	83
Amelia Mobsby	84
Gemma Martin	84
Hannah Plowman	85
Jenny Valentine	86
Thomas Kingscott	86
Ben Hunt	87
Saoirse Koch	87

St Joseph's RC Combined School, Poole

Stefan Brown	88
Victoria Lawlor	88

Georgina McLaughlin	89
Emily Fisk	89
Lydia Gibbons	90
John Adkins	90
Claire Frigot	91
Jade Cadby	91
Brendan Byrne	92
Elizabeth Martin	92
Ben Absolom	93
Benito Viola	94
Anthony Matthews	94
Michael Godden	95
Domenico Salvia	95
James Tucker	96
Ryan Trowbridge	96
Ashley Dunford	97
Sophie Angell	97
Max Forward	97
Freya Gill	98
Mariette Trott	98
Aine Wood	98
Lewis Connor	99
Megan Davis	99
David Rudenko	99

St Michael's CE Primary School, Bournemouth

Charlotte Clarke	100
Charlotte Marshall	100
Alice Chatfield	101
Alice Ivory	101
Chenice Manning	102
Kate Dawson	103
Jodie Lydia Radulovitch	104
Michael Goodrich	104
Taranjeet Lall	105
Arabella Da Costa	105
Grace Nevill	106
Craig Hancock	106

Katya Rose	107
Ross Welsh	107
Yolanda Jacob	108
Sandra Pita	108
Lucy Jones	109
Holly Nicholson	110
Andrew Mason	110
Jemma Derby	111
Nina Luminati	112

St Thomas Garnet's School, Bournemouth

Emma Jones	113
Rachel Gillings	114
Natalie Wedge	114
Peter Landi	115
Todd Lewis	115
Rayna Chauhan	116
Kimberley Sobisch	116
Louis Luke	117
Oliver Porter	118
Jennifer Law	118
Sam Plank	119
Joshua Bowmen	119
Natalie Rondeau	120
Carina Hall-Nicolls	120
Ross Browne	121
Brookeleah Gossling	122
Ryan Lewis	122
Rebecca Murphy	123
Emily King	123
Catherine Hixson	124
Bryony Cook	124
Maeve Orla Dunne	125
Kristy O'Donnell	126
Harry Leedham	126
Connor Groves-Waters	127
Ben Waller	128
Alex Thayne	128

Kapil Chauhan	129
Julian Osei-Bonsu	129
Paeris Giles	130
Connor Rockey	131
Tanja Wagner	132
David Passmore	132
William Porter	133
Georgia Hill	133
Iniubong Udoeyop	134
Mark Leedham	134
Jana Browne	135
Jordan Norris	135
India Hall	136
Hannah Elcock	136
Rachel Dingley	137
Hannah Pickup	137
George Soan	138

The Epiphany School

Nathan Watkins	138
Natasha Daysh	139
Aaron Trowbridge	139
Mandy Cronk	140
Simone Claire Vibert	140
Zack Reed	141
Alex Lee	142
Benjamin Clayton	142
Sasha Jones	143
Emily Apps	144
Edita Parkinson	144
Hannah Featherstone	145
Grant Wells	146
William Handford	146
Samuel Walkling-Talbot	147
Chloe Runnacles	147
Natalie Dyke	148
Jade Evans	148
Natalie George	149

Catherine Lee-Smith	149
Hannah Dibden	150
Mary Johnstone	151
Claudia Poole	152
Elizabeth Kimber	152
Jessica Saracino	153
Genevieve Martin	153
Aron Shute	154
Natasha Triggs	154
Jason Everitt	155
Sian Burton	155
Charlotte Harwood	156
Ella Owen	156
Zoe Escott	157
Francesca Simpson-Rathbone	157
Samantha Fear	158
Lawrence Warner Green	159
Gemma Sandell	159
Leanna Bartlett	160
Charlotte Cleere	160
Kate Sidwick	161
Lauren Gatcum	161
Stephanie Duggan	161
Alexandra Lauren Ridout	162
Shaun Burbidge	162
Katy Brothers	163
Jake Ashley Carton	163
Sophia Moorehouse	164
Adam Dean	164
Zachary Bradley	164
Naomi Davies	165
Zara Baxter	165
Zak Sutcliffe	165
Lewis Paul Vincent	166
Zoë Emma Beale	166
Adam Proudley	166

Upton Junior School

Michael Homer	167
Stephanie Stokes	168
Zoë Swinburn	169
Sandeep Marwaha	170
Ashleigh Pegg	170
Kym Gibbs	171
Daniel Rose	172
Jenny Wigmore	172
Faye Mitchell	173
Ellen House	173
Shontelle Young	174
Harriet Davis	174
Nikki Turner	175
Hannah Powis	176
Matt Mosley	176
Matthew Knight	177
Chris Emerson	177
Kathryn Cullen	178
Kristopher Jones	178
Danny Hudson	179
Rebecca Pierce	180
Sam Sweeney	180
Robert Hatchard	181
Jessica Herron	182
Lara Maley	182
David Armstrong	183
Liam McCabe	184
Jack Greenslade	184
Amie Borg	185
Danny Agar	185
Tiffany Atwill	186
Alicia Wright	187
Chloe Lloyd	188
Daniel Jackson	188
Tim Cottis	189
Katie Jolly	189
Aaron Palmer	190

Rachel Murphy	190
Liam Packer	191
Rebekah Campbell	192
Georgina Ann Turner	192
James Fleischer	193
Melissa Jones	193
Samuel Ball	194
Gemma West	194
Joanne Hodd	195
Victoria Gladden	196
Leigh Marie Evans	196
Jade Holloway	197
Jade Mary Starmer	197
Kate Sanders	198
Claire Orchard	198
Claire Stokes	199
Laura Stockley	199
Travers Gardner	200
Claire Thomson	200
Lara Hackney	201
Rachel Hewitt	202
Robin Peacock	203
Hannah Bolt	204
Killion McKenzie	204
Ryan Birch	205
Dylan Smith	206

The Poems

IF I WERE A BEAR

If I were a bear
And a big bear too,
I shouldn't much care
If it froze or snew.
I shouldn't much mind,
If it snowed or froze -
I'd be all fur-lined
With a coat like his!
For I'd have fur boots and a brown fur wrap
And brown fur knickers and a big fur cap.
I'd have a fur muffle-ruff to cover my jaws
And brown fur mittens on my big brown paws.
With a big brown furry-down up to my head,
I'd sleep all the winter in a big fur bed.

Lauren Wareham (10)
Alderney County Middle School

THE MUMMY'S CURSE

Once upon a time, in a far, faraway land,
A dry and dusty desert stretched as far
As a dry and dusty eye could see.
On the edge of that dry and dusty desert
The mystical monuments of an ancient civilisation
Shimmered in the hazy heat of the midday sun.
Deep in the heart of a mighty pyramid,
Lay the tomb of an ancient family of kings
And in that dark and silent tomb,
A royal family of mummies
Lay sleeping through the centuries . . .

Alex Buckland (9)
Alderney County Middle School

SEASONS

It was a cold, blustery day in the middle of Jan,
I couldn't wait for the summer to get a tan.
In winter, we can't go out much, so we watch lots of telly,
In the summer we can go to the beach and run in the sea,
Right up to your belly.
I much prefer summer than winter, there's much more to do,
We go bike riding, the beach, or the forest and hear the cows moo.
In summer a picnic is great on a hot, sunny day,
You can go for a walk in the forest and you don't have to pay.
In August it's my birthday and I will be eleven,
My brother, Harry is only seven.
I don't mind the snow, the sun, but dislike the rain,
It gets you wet and stops you playing outside, it's such a pain.
Spring is nice when it starts to warm up,
When leaves grow on the trees and bulbs pop up.
In autumn the leaves start to fall and then it's winter again, that's all.

Sammy Terrell (10)
Alderney County Middle School

MY MUM

My mum is kind,
My mum is pretty,
My mum is cuddly,
My mum is generous,
My mum is funny,
My mum smells like a rose,
My mum shouts,
My mum moans.

Danielle Clark (8)
Alderney County Middle School

FEELING FRIGHTENED

F eeling frightened like a rolling apple,
R unning away from my scary thing,
I gnoring my fear is not good,
G rinning and saying there's nothing wrong,
H iding in the dark, makes my friends scared,
T here's a spider, *aaaggh!* I'm frightened of spiders!
E ven little ones,
N o one knows how I feel,
E ven though they are scared of something,
D o they understand me?

Jodie Lillington (9)
Alderney County Middle School

LONELY

Lost and lonely in the park,
Everyone's gone, left behind.
I'm lost in the park,
Come back everyone!
I'm lying on the grass,
I wish someone was here,
Come here please!
But nobody hears,
I'm lonely.

Sophie Mudge (9)
Alderney County Middle School

THE ANIMAL POEM

There's a dog in the house
eating all the meat.

There's a rabbit in the garden
eating all the lettuce.

There's a dolphin in the sea
eating all the fish.

There's a bear in the woods
eating all the honey.

There's a horse in the stable
eating all the hay.

There's a fox in the den
eating all the rabbits.

There's a hamster in a cage
eating all the mix.

There's a squirrel in the tree
eating all the acorns.

There's a cow in the field
eating all the grass.

There's a shark in the sea
eating me!

Kayleigh Collbourne (10)
Alderney County Middle School

MY BROTHER, AARON

My brother, Aaron, he is kind,
He is helpful and he shouts,
He is funny like a cheeky monkey,
He is generous

And he is a great joker,
He is a great footballer
And he helps me when I'm stuck,
He is great at sports,
That's my brother, Aaron.

Kyle Stacey (8)
Alderney County Middle School

My Mum

My mum is like a beautiful rose,
A lovely princess,
She is kind,
But watch out . . .
She shouts!
But she calms down
And then . . .
She's cuddly, lovely and loveable again.

Anastasia Day (8)
Alderney County Middle School

My Mum

My mum is pretty,
She smells like a rose,
She likes to go shopping
And buy lots of clothes.
She sometimes gets sad
And feels quite grumpy,
When she is cooking,
She makes it all lumpy!

Victoria Bridgeman (8)
Alderney County Middle School

THE ADVENTURES OF ISABELLE

I sabelle is not scared of anyone.
S nakes, poisonous ones, I'm still not scared
A nd she likes football.
B rothers, I hate them.
E nter my territory and you'll be dead.
L ocation is a sunny, deserted place.
L itres of cherryade to drink.
E xpeditions are what I like.

Isabelle Mitchell (8)
Alderney County Middle School

A NEW DAY

The silence of the night is broken by the church bells,
they chime five times.
The foxes slink away after rummaging in bins,
the badgers hide away.
A chink in the curtains shows a faint tendril of light,
a streak of crimson.
A lonely dog somewhere out there, barks momentarily.
I snuggle down in my bed.
I suddenly hear what I've been waiting for -
The first bird singing,
it heralds the beginning of the dawn chorus,
now many join in.
The whine of the milk float travels slowly towards us;
the clink of bottles on the doorstep.
A car starts up nearby and joins another on the road,
other sounds join in.
I leap out of bed to share this brand new day
with everyone.

Dylan Frost (11)
All Saints CE Primary School

TED TREASURE

One day,
He went away.

My ted called Fred,
He was down the other end of the bed!
I cried and cried,
But he never replied.
So I went to look for him,
Despite everything.
I decided to make haste,
Something grabbed my waist!
It was only my pyjama case.
I heard a rattling moan,
It sounded like a skeleton shaking a bone!
But it was only the TV,
Showing a scary movie!
Finally I got there and discovered my ted,
My most treasured possession,
Hiding under the bed.

Cicely Clasby (11)
All Saints CE Primary School

NIGHT-TIME DREAM

Hidden treasure, strange vision.
Perplexing colours, drifting away.
Sinking into the deep, dark night.
Eternal happiness is your destiny.
A hushed, empty world.
Unthinkable answers to
Unthinkable questions.
Only you can find the treasure.

Laurence Atchison (10)
All Saints CE Primary School

HIDE AND SEEK

It was my turn to seek,
Everyone had rushed off,
Screaming and yelling in delight.
Then all was quiet,
Silence, nothing and no one moved.
'I'm coming!' I yelled
And began my search.
In the greenhouse? No, only seed trays.
Behind the fir tree? Tall and bushy.
In the old barn? No, only hay and giant cobwebs.
By the side of the big gate? Brown and sturdy.
I had searched high and low,
But there was still one place where I hadn't hunted,
The garden shed, brown and battered.
I opened the door, the rusty hinges creaked.
Suddenly a sea of smiles greeted me.
'You found us!' they cheered.

Emma Murcer (10)
All Saints CE Primary School

A DEATH SENTENCE

AIDS, a death sentence;
slow, lingering, painful.
Scientists working on a cure;
chemicals, test tubes, jars.
Substances, medicines, anything
to prevent further deterioration.
Euphoria, the day comes when a
breakthrough is discovered.
There in a test tube, a hidden treasure,
finally unlocked by man.

Andrew Read (11)
All Saints CE Primary School

VIVID TREASURE

It had been glorious,
A lazy day, too hot to move.
Bumblebees buzzing,
Birds listlessly soaring high.

I moved my chair round,
Facing west to follow the sun.
From bright blue,
Now the sky subtly changing colour.

Purple streaks invading,
A lonely cloud edged with silver.
Now introducing crimson,
Touching my surroundings with a rosy glow.

As the sun sinks,
Preparing to illuminate the southern hemisphere,
Distant objects
Turn into stark silhouettes.

Blazing, burning, fiery,
The sky tries to hold the melted copper sun.
I blink weary eyes
And watch twilight battling with sunset.

I caught a glimpse
Of a second in time that lasted half an hour.
I still sit in my chair,
Contented and in awe of yet another stunning sunset.

Mark Capon (10)
All Saints CE Primary School

Rabbit

Cardboard boxes cover my bedroom floor
filled with precious belongings.
But I'm only looking for one.

My oldest, smelliest, shabbiest possession.
The toy rabbit as old as me,
present from Dad.

I open all the boxes to start searching.
Toys fly in all directions.
It's got to be here.

I know it got packed, it was a priority,
but not in my boxes, obviously.
Where is my rabbit?

Settling into a new house can be unsettling.
My family are kind and search with me,
they try to reassure me.

Mum finds and opens the box marked *Kitchen*.
She pulls out the kettle and teapot,
she pulls out mugs.

Mum delves into the depths of the box.
Finds spoons, tea, milk and sugar,
pulls out my rabbit by his ear.

Tim Bailey (10)
All Saints CE Primary School

For All Of Eternity

My very first turn of gazing upon this sunset
shall be desired for all of eternity.
A soft mix of blue drifts into a vibrant pink.
Enchanting colours illuminating your mind.
Light red melting into a creamy orange.

The souls of the trees running off into the silence of the night,
as if a single penny is being lowered into a money box.
My turn of looking upon this golden ball of fire is over,
for someone else shall gaze upon
this hidden treasure tomorrow.

Hephzibah Watts (10)
All Saints CE Primary School

THE JOURNEY TO THE END OF THE BED

I lost my teddy three weeks ago,
He's down at the end of the bed.
So I decided to look for him,
But that was a terrible mistake.

I began my journey on the feather sea,
It took me ages to cross.
Then I embarked on the pillow planes,
The blanket bandits were a pain.

I had to climb the cover mountains,
It took me days to pass.
Then I spied cover city,
Where I guessed teddy would be.

I saw my ted on the rack,
His eyes begged me to save him.
I tackled the guards
And knocked them out.

I'd got my ted - I'd rescued him.
My treasured companion had returned.

Sam Buckland (10)
All Saints CE Primary School

MY TREASURE

My lonely and unhappy walk
had brought me to this wild place.
Beware! No admittance the signs had said,
This quarry is dangerous.
The bitter wind sent low, dark clouds
scudding across the sky.
It moaned across the top of the quarry.
I felt like moaning too,
growing up is hard.
A few feet below the edge
was an object; a large crumpled up piece of material,
an old cape or cloak.
Curiosity overcame crossness.
I carefully climbed down to look
and crawled back up with my prize.
I shook out the cloak,
a little telescope in ebony and brass,
as old as the hills with thick glass ends.
I had a very peculiar feeling
as I peered into it.
I didn't see what was in front of me.
I saw myself, a husband, children, family.
The future! I could see into the future!
It looked cosy, contented, happy,
something to look forward to.
What an amazing find, better than a fortune
in gold, silver or riches.

Casey Brown (10)
All Saints CE Primary School

WHITE TREASURE

Heavy skies promise
Long awaited snow.
I sit on the window ledge,
Waiting for my first glimpse,
I've sat patiently for a long time.

My breath creates patterns
On the windowpane.
Something soft and small
Drifts delicately down.
I tense with excitement and expectation.

A stray snowflake.
I look out and up.
Wisps of snow,
Millions, swirling in the wind,
This is it! My first experience of snow.

Gloves and scarf on,
Wellington boots on.
I rush outside
And look up to the sky.
Snowflakes gently settle on my eyelashes and nose.

There is almost no sound,
Only a wet pattering.
Branches, hedges and leaves
Are dusted white.
I feel exhilarated, so I dance in the snow.

Natasha Wiltshire (10)
All Saints CE Primary School

TREASURED FRIENDSHIP

F riends, people you can trust
R ather then be wary. Always
I nstep with me. We
E njoy having fun. Always there in times of
N eed. Never
D oubting you.
S ympathetic and kind-
H earted.
I ntimate and agreeable.
P eople who are loving. Treasured forever.

Jessica Winsper (10)
All Saints CE Primary School

SUNRISE

The sun was rising,
The people slept,
Darkened room, dark streets.
Slowly, over the hills,
The sun's rays burst,
Onto the sleeping town.
Gold, rouge, yellow,
Light fell onto the dark land
And then I realised what the treasure really was.

Ben Brotherwood (10)
All Saints CE Primary School

THE WINTER'S NIGHT

The silence of the darkness,
The cold winter trees,
The silver of the moonlight,
The rustle of the leaves,
The movement of a fox tail,
The deep, black sky,
The trickle of a golden stream,
Flowing slowly by,
The iciness of the layer
Forming on the grass,
Glowing in the movement,
Looking just like brass,
Jack Frost has come again,
On this cold, wintry night,
Running over the treetops,
Spreading a beautiful, silvery light.

Susie Coreth (10)
Knighton House School

TIME

Time.
Time goes by. That second shall never be again.
Time. The wind hurrying the clouds across the sky.
Time goes by. Can you remember what happened five minutes ago?

Time. The acorn grows into a huge oak.
Time goes by. The pages of the book are turned from first to last.

Time. Morning melts into night.
Time goes by and the baby will die.

Memmi Rasmussen (11)
Knighton House School

SHIPWRECK

Deep under the crashing waves, far, faraway,
The skeleton of a ship lies
Quiet and desolate, with no one aboard; like the silent world around it.

In the hold are glittering treasures of numerous wealth,
You may try to find them, yet fail.

Inside the galley are half-finished sausages and grog and beans!
But in the captain's quarters, a monstrous sight.
A skeleton, covered with disintegrating cloth,
Has been made a home of.

Surely this could not happen under the stars and the froth,
On such a peaceful night as this?

But now the man-eater has risen again, the terror of the seas,
Waiting, ever waiting, for the food of its dreams.

India Lewis (10)
Knighton House School

ESCAPE

She twisted round, up and down
Turning this way and that
Bending here, bending there
Moving swiftly without a care

But then she scuttled away
Never to be seen
Up the wall, in the corner
Jumping beam to beam

On the floor, under the door
She was gone, gone forever more.

Rebecca Sutton (10)
Knighton House School

SOARING HIGH UP ABOVE

I find myself soaring high up above,
With wings like a dove,
I'm the symbol of love
And just with a shove,
I was pushed up to God,
Who replied with a nod,
'Come and have tea,
But please don't worry.'
Then I woke up
And ever since then,
I've believed in one god,
The one I had tea with,
High up above!

Sophie Thorpe (10)
Knighton House School

HORSES

Galloping along the seashore,
Their tails and manes flying like the wind.

Cantering through the woods,
Kicking up mud on the way.

Trotting along a dusty road,
Neighing and snorting at any kind of mammal.

Walking in the paddock,
Tired and restless and eating its hay.

In the stable lying down,
Dropping off into a deep, dreamy sleep.

Milly Donaldson (11)
Knighton House School

MONKEY

Monkey swinging through the trees,
Then he stops to survey the scene,
Cautiously he climbs to the ground.
Why is he hunched over something?
What has he found?
Is it ripe berries, fruit or nuts?
Then the monkey turns to scoot,
He has found four hunters in hunting suits.

The hunters turn round and begin to run,
Each of them carrying a big, black gun.
Firing them here and there,
Three bullets pierce the monkey's hair.
He falls from the trees into a deserted bed,
Blood is seeping from the wounds,
He is *dead!*

Emily Girkins (10)
Knighton House School

SPIDER

Spider is my pony
Pretty and bright
Intelligent and useful
Walking in the moonlight

White is she
When the mud is off
'Oh,' she says
With a little cough.

Iona Woods (11)
Knighton House School

SUMMER

A cool wind whistles through the trees,
It's only a pleasant summer breeze.
Rabbits hop to and fro,
Only they know where they'll go.
Golden corn the field mice eat,
As well as barley, nuts and wheat.

In the wood the bluebird sings,
From its small beak to tiny wings.
Behind the shed the fox glowers,
At something beyond some pretty flowers.
Children laughing, are at play,
To help pass the day away.

Night has crept up and fell,
But watch inside the little dell,
Because the badger will come out
And he'll snuffle all about.
Everybody's gone to their beds,
To rest all their tired heads.

Jenny McCavitt (11)
Knighton House School

MONSTERS

M onsters are big, frightening and bold,
O ld monsters only come out in the cold.
N astily they plan their plot,
S itting in their caves of decay and rot.
T onight they will be in
E very house, hiding in the dim.
R avenous monsters will be out tonight,
S neaking around to give you a fright.

Eliza Sketchley (10)
Knighton House School

THE SEASONS

Autumn

Brown leaves on the ground,
Crunch, crunch as you walk around.
Autumn time has begun,
Children have lots of fun.

Winter

The chilly winds, now they blow,
Sending a forecast of snow.
Hats and scarves you have to wear,
When you are going out there.

Spring

Snowdrops and daffodils come,
Then comes the beautiful sun.
Freshly-born lambs here and there,
Eating grass without a care.

Summer

The sun comes shining bright,
Just like a pure ball of light.
Time to go and have some fun,
Just before winter comes.

Polly Meyer (10)
Knighton House School

MISSING SCHOOL

Oh no, it's my
First day in
Year Four.

I wonder if
Mrs Walker
Will be strict?

I walk into the
Classroom, all these
Eyes stare at me.

I feel like a
Shrimp surrounded
By sharks.

Work, work all day
Long, it feels like
Ages.

Wow, whoopee, the bell
Has rung!
I jump out of my seat.

Kicking, shouting, I
Barge to the door and
Run as fast as I can
Down the corridor.

Outside, the wind gusts
Through the trees
And my hair is
All on end.

Pippa Beard (8)
Motcombe Grange School

HORRID HOMEWORK!

At 3.40pm the bell rings,
Everybody sings,
Mrs Walker
Gives out the homework,
We all look grumpy.

Children rushing down the stairs,
Everybody jumping on the squares,
We all get excited,
That it is the end of school,
But we have to do our homework.

I get home and settle in,
My mum forces me
To do my homework,
I shout,
'Horrid homework!'

Rebecca Antill (9)
Motcombe Grange School

COOKS

The cooks
Do lovely
Dinners.

Flan and
Jacket potato
Yum, yum.

My mum
Always asks
Me

'What have
You had for
Dinner?'

'My favourite
Can you
Guess?'

Hooray, back
To school
On Monday.

Georgina Alice Stopford (8)
Motcombe Grange School

HORRIFIC HOMEWORK

3.40pm, it's the end of the day,
Our class all shout, 'Hip, hip, hooray!'
Mrs Walker comes in with a pile of sheets
Oh guess what it is?
I have a little peep
It's miserable maths!
Mrs Walker puts her glasses on the end of her nose
And shouts, 'Homework books out!'
We all look on the board
The board says
You have marvellous maths
Horrific history
And remarkable reading
I said in my head
She's wrong!

Eliza Hamer (8)
Motcombe Grange School

SO ANNOYING!

When I came back to school
One day as I had been
On holiday, the most annoying
Things had happened
On the day I'd been away
Our teacher had been off sick
And my class went on
A school trip!

My best friend had a party
And she had lots of Smarties
Next-door's chickens escaped
And the school cooks made
Them a pellet cake!

At home it had been really boring
I was doing loads of snoring
And now I realise I
Really would like
To go back to
School again.

Henrietta Dillon (9)
Motcombe Grange School

END OF SCHOOL

The door swings open
Children rushing home
Shouting, jumping, running
Whoosh, the leaves are flying
Children twirling in a hurricane way
Children rushing to their parents
Children running off
Children saying 'Hip, hip, hooray!'

The sound fades away, away, away
Cars start their engines
Everyone's gone home
The school stands all alone.

Leo Dexter (8)
Motcombe Grange School

ALL ABOUT BIRDS

I wish I could fly
Up high in the sky
Like a bird with beautiful wings
I love how a bird sings
Like a golden eagle
Or a beautiful grey and white seagull
Not a long, floppy-eared beagle
They are beautiful those birds
I wish I could speak in birds' words
And fly from tree to tree
Or over the sea
Watch children play
And understand what they say
Would you like to be
A beautiful bird?

Beatrice Herbert (8)
Motcombe Grange School

VERY LOUD!

The school bell rang
A few people sang
We said, 'Good afternoon'
School's been, done and gone
An echo of loudness travelling down the stairs
Some people talking in pairs
Stamp! Stamp! go the feet on the stairs
Children rushing to their pegs
And grabbing their coats
Running like mad
To their mums and dads!

Alice McKeith (8)
Motcombe Grange School

MY GRAN

My gran is as caring as can be,
She's as cuddly as a furry bear,
Her eyes sparkle like a dazzling star,
That are always there to stare.

Her skin is as crinkly as an autumn leaf,
She has a good sense of humour,
Her cheeks are pink and rosy,
She wears wonderful perfume.

She walks like the wavy sea,
She snores like the wind blowing gently,
I love my gran,
She does everything for me,
The best thing is that
She will always love me.

Annabel Lane (8)
St Andrew's Primary School, Weymouth

MY NANNY!

I love my nanny (she is a caring granny!)
She is as nice as can be,
With skin as crinkly as a tree.

I love my nanny (she is cool as can be!)
She is quiet as a mouse
And as big as a house.

I love my nanny (she loves me!)
Her eyes are sparkling stars
And she likes chocolate bars.

I love my nanny (she is beautiful as can be!)
Her favourite drink is a cup of tea
And she loves to hear some bees.

I love my nanny (she is lovely as a cake!)
She loves gardening and putting flowers in,
The dead flowers she throws in the bin.

Victoria McNern (9)
St Andrew's Primary School, Weymouth

FIREWORKS

Rockets shooting up and down,
Catherine wheels rotating round,
Roman candles whizzing,
Sparklers fizzing,
Fountains exploding,
Sparkling silver, illuminated yellow,
Zooming into space.

Bryony Bratchell (8)
St Andrew's Primary School, Weymouth

WINTER

W indy days
I cy nights
N ice warm fires
T elling everybody winter is here
E verything is white
R obins come out to play.

Lauren Bourne (8)
St Andrew's Primary School, Weymouth

WINTER

W hen I look out the window
I see crumbling snow everywhere
N o leaves on the trees
T ime for summer to sleep
E verything is white and sparkling
R obins flying above us.

Domonic Sorokopud (8)
St Andrew's Primary School, Weymouth

WINTER

W hite snow, great!
I t is never this cold.
N orth wind is coming, I must keep warm.
T ell everybody winter is here.
E verything is white and glimmering.
R oast turkey soon, *yum!*

Chloe Drew (8)
St Andrew's Primary School, Weymouth

My Gran

My gran is kind and loving
She takes good care of me
She tells me lots of stories
And invites me round to tea

Her face is old and wrinkled
Her hair is curly and grey
Her eyes are like glittering stars
Her teeth are from Mars!

My gran is the best gran ever
She does lots of things for me
My gran's good and helpful
She takes me to the sea.

Jennie Martin (8)
St Andrew's Primary School, Weymouth

My Gran

My gran is kind and loving
She takes good care of me
She shows me lots of knitting
And takes me to the sea

Her face is old and wrinkled
Her hair is soft and grey
Her eyes are like sapphires
Her teeth are like the Milky Way

My gran is the best gran ever
She does lots of things for me
She takes me to the Nothe
She loves me you see.

Rosie Prior (8)
St Andrew's Primary School, Weymouth

MY GRAN

My gran is kind and loving
She takes good care of me
She never tells me lies
She takes me out to sea

Her face is old and wrinkled
Her eyes are like sapphires
Her teeth are like the sun in the day
Her hair is very soft, in a way

My gran is never bad
And she helps me when I'm sad
She's the best gran I've ever seen
Her heart beats just like a dream

That's all I can say
Well, her heart still beats today
I'm glad that it's true, that she loves me
And I say, 'Gran, I love you too!'

Victoria Browne (8)
St Andrew's Primary School, Weymouth

MY GRANDAD

I love my grandad
he is kind and lovely
he gets me sweets
he is very nice
he has grey hair around a paper bag face
he has a walking stick and a hearing aid
green jumper and grey trousers are the clothes he wears
I love him so much
I could live with him.

James Almond (8)
St Andrew's Primary School, Weymouth

Holding My Baby

Holding my beautiful, cuddly, new baby
Makes me feel very grown up.
I also feel worried, she is so fragile.
She is soft and cute,
Wriggling, tossing her head,
Dribbling down her chin,
I love my smiling, new baby.

Zoey Peppin (8)
St Andrew's Primary School, Weymouth

Winter

W   onderful white snow
I   cy, cold air
N   ights are so snowy
T   rees are so bare
E   verything in my garden is frozen
R   ivers start melting when the sun comes out.

Chelsea Ratcliffe (8)
St Andrew's Primary School, Weymouth

Fireworks

Glittering yellow and dark green sparks,
Circling, whizzing, colourful Catherine wheels,
Banging, crashing, exploding fireworks,
Terrible smoky smell!
Whizzing, whirling, zooming, exploding,
Flying into the night sky.

Christopher Kitching (9)
St Andrew's Primary School, Weymouth

THE MAGIC BOX

I will put in my box,
The silk of a chestnut shell,
The fur of a soft leopard,
The shimmer of a shiny dolphin.
I will put in my box,
The ripple of chocolate sauce,
The Queen on a skateboard,
Scarecrow harvesting, farmer standing in a field.

I will put in my box,
A month old baby talking, grown man crying,
A dog miaowing, a cat ruffing,
Grass on the washing line, clothes on the grass.

My box is shiny, with polished jewels,
The rubies shine as the sun goes down,
The key is a star, to all living things.

I shall skate the world till people are mixed,
There shall be no war, no fighting,
The world will be a better place!

Steven Rockett (11)
St Andrew's Primary School, Weymouth

FIREWORKS

Crimson gold and shimmering silver,
Dazzling, shooting, bolting, bursting,
Whistling, thundering, fizzing,
Burning, smoky and fiery,
Energetically darting, twirling, whirling,
Shooting into the dark night sky.

Madeleine Puleston (8)
St Andrew's Primary School, Weymouth

KITE

I
Slowly move
Through the trees,
Carried by a lovely breeze,
As I drift through the air, I
Don't even care if I get
Stuck in a tree but
When I come down
And fall to
The
Ground
I
Want
To
Do
It
Again.

Danielle Green (8)
St Andrew's Primary School, Weymouth

HOLDING MY BABY BROTHER

When my brother was a baby he was quite wriggly,
I fed him with his bottle,
He cried a lot, I felt so grown up.

I felt nervous and scared,
I would *love* my mum to have another one,
When my brother cried, I held him,
I love my brother so much!

Lisa Harrington (9)
St Andrew's Primary School, Weymouth

My Grandma

My grandma is as kind as can be
When she sleeps she is as still as an oak tree

Her eyes are like the deep blue ocean
When she coughs it is like a magic potion

When she sleeps she is as silent as a mouse
I love going to her warm, cosy house

My grandma is very funny
She likes to give me toast and honey

Her hair is grey and curly, like sheep's wool
When I go swimming, she swims in the pool

The best thing about her is that she loves me
And she sometimes takes me to the wonderful sea.

Rachel Sykes (9)
St Andrew's Primary School, Weymouth

Holding The Baby

I'm having a photo holding my baby sister,
What a zone for photo disaster!
She's gurgling, spitting, smelly and drooling and *cute!*
I hold her still on my lap,
As she takes a little nap!
Snap! Off goes the camera -
And the kid too!
Nothing I can do!
We put away the camera,
She giggles,
'Not too bad for a baby!' I say!

Amelia Bull (9)
St Andrew's Primary School, Weymouth

THE FOUR SEASONS

First is winter,
Cold, snowy winter,
Lakes are frozen
And robins come to play.

When winter has gone,
Spring is here,
The blossoms come out
And the lambs play.

In summer frogs are born,
First as tadpoles with a tail,
Then with legs,
Croaking on the lily pads.

Then comes autumn with crunchy leaves,
Out come the woodlice, snails and bees,
Leaves are falling slowly,
Falling ready for winter.

Ellen Norman (9)
St Andrew's Primary School, Weymouth

MY GRANDMA

My grandma says on a Sunday,
'Let's go and get a paper.'
We get The Sun for Grandpa
And we get some sweets for Monday.

My grandma lets me watch TV in bed,
My grandma is the best.
My grandma is kind and funny,
She helped me when I bumped my head.

Stuart Felstead (9)
St Andrew's Primary School, Weymouth

SNAKE CARE

Most people say they are slimy
But they are not
My friend has a pet one
It's been in my hair
Even though it's not very clean
I wish I had one
Probably a corn snake, so nice
I love snakes, even though they eat mice
Creamy and brown
They grow up to nine feet long
Slithering so fast
I wish I had one
They feed on dead mice (that's disgusting!)
But *I love them!*

Sapphira Pratt (9)
St Andrew's Primary School, Weymouth

MY GRANDAD

My grandad is a lovely man
He has a wrinkly face
He sometimes walks a distance
He sometimes walks a pace

He's always helping with the dinner
His cat is much, much thinner
My grandad is the strangest man on Earth
That's why he can surf
I love my grandad.

Robyn Welford (8)
St Andrew's Primary School, Weymouth

HOLDING THE BABY

Mum's new baby is cuddly and sweet
    She's gurgling
I feel nervous
    I'm holding her
I'm scared I might drop her
    She's very sleepy
Oh no, I hope she doesn't start crying

I feel quite safe now
    She's giggling
She thinks I'm funny
    I feel grown up
But quite worried.

Cerys Jones (8)
St Andrew's Primary School, Weymouth

STARS

Little tiny rocks up high,
Twinkling brightly in the sky.

Glittering colours of the rainbow,
Glowing high and glowing low.

Shooting stars with a dazzling spark,
Only appear when it is dark.

Wishing upon each little star,
Wonderful things they really are.

Zoë Day (9)
St Andrew's Primary School, Weymouth

FIREWORKS

Flashing blue and light red
Shooting stars and falling petals
Screeching and screaming
Burning gunpowder, smoking fire
Hurtling into space, darting around
Up and up
Then showering down.

Philip Cole (8)
St Andrew's Primary School, Weymouth

FIREWORKS

Crimson gold and shimmering silver,
Exploding dynamite,
Erupting volcano,
Burning fire,
Zooming rockets,
Into the dark night sky.

Warren Hicks (8)
St Andrew's Primary School, Weymouth

WINTER

W hen I felt winter was here
I t was very cold
N ights were growing longer
T oday it's Christmas Day
E very child has some gifts
R unning and playing in the cold snow.

Benjamin Woodland (8)
St Andrew's Primary School, Weymouth

MY CAT

My cat is black,
He sleeps all day,
He's rather old you see.

My cat is black,
He lies by the fire,
He likes it warm you see.

My cat is black,
His whiskers are white,
He's nearly seventeen you see.

My cat is black,
He's very clever,
He's been here longer than me you see.

I love my cat.

Francesca Guarraci (7)
St Andrew's Primary School, Weymouth

MY NEW BABY BROTHER

I'm excited about my new, cuddly baby brother,
I have a beautiful, wonderful baby on my lap,
I want a photo, I say and another.

You're small and sweet,
All cuddly and cute,
With very little, tiny feet.

Oh baby boy all dressed in blue,
So tiny and small,
Too good to be true.

Sam Shurey (9)
St Andrew's Primary School, Weymouth

HOLDING THE BABY

Holding my baby makes me happy
But I'm frightened
With a soaking nappy
He wriggles about

The fat thing is snoring
Blowing bubbles
And very boring

He smells like fish
His nappy needs changing
He smashed my dish
He is crying.

Jordan Emburey (9)
St Andrew's Primary School, Weymouth

WHAT A LOT OF KITTENS

K itten is black and white,
I t is a playful cat,
T he cat likes to play with wool,
T he cat has six kittens,
E veryone likes the kittens,
N ow they will keep all of the kittens.

S ometimes the kittens are rude,
T hey sell one kitten
A nd keep the other five,
R ocky bar is their best food.

Emma Taylor (7)
St Andrew's Primary School, Weymouth

ROMAN TOWNS

R omans build their own houses,
O ne day the volcano erupted,
M ore and more ash and lava came out
A nd more and more people died,
N one had their own baths but only the rich.

T he Gladiators fought till death,
O nly the rich went to school,
W hen they go on holiday they stay in hotels,
N o one served in Pompeii,
S o that was the end of that!

Verity Witt (8)
St Andrew's Primary School, Weymouth

RAIN AND THUNDER

Rain and thunder in the night
Making a dark sky glow so bright
Pitter-patter, hear the rain
Beating loudly on a windowpane
Rain and thunder, hear it roar
Louder and louder
I can bear it no more
Then all is still
Not a noise to be heard
Except me waking up to the chirping of birds.

Grace Passoni (7)
St Andrew's Primary School, Weymouth

MY MAGIC BOX

I will put in my box

The shimmer and shine of a shooting star
The buzz of a buzzing bee
The touch of a baby's bottom

I will put in my box

The fragrance of French perfume
The whistling and wailing of the wind
The tangy taste of Doritos

I will put in my box

The last word of a great aunt
The tantrum of a two-year-old
The oozing sound of mud

I will put in my box

A dog with a miaow
A cat with a bark
A hare with a slimy body

My box is fashioned from silver velvet
With stars on the lid and figures in the corners
The hinges are made from the silk inside a chestnut shell

I shall dance in my box
In the moonlit night
Then swim with the dolphins in the Jamaican sea.

Amy Small (11)
St Andrew's Primary School, Weymouth

THE MAGIC BOX

I will put in the box
The sound of sizzling bacon in a pan
The taste of crunchy, soft potatoes on Sunday
The smell of petrol on a windy day

I will put in the box
The touch of a baby's fingers in my hand
The sight of a baby eating his tea
The smell of bacon when I'm in bed

I will put in the box
A dog with a man on a lead
A polar bear in Australia
A fried egg in the oven

I will put in the box
A piano playing a human
An aeroplane flying a man
A mouse chasing a cat

My box is made from sponge cake
With a key of strawberry lace
Its locks are fruit pastille body parts

I shall eat my box all day
But it will just grow back
So I will eat it forever and ever.

Barney Moss (10)
St Andrew's Primary School, Weymouth

THE MAGIC BOX

I will put in the box
The howl of the wild wind
The scent of a wonderful rose
The taste of taramasalata

I will put in the box
The brush of a wet octopus
A slimy salmon just been eaten
The colour of the Greek sea in the sunlight

I will put in the box
A bull on a lead
And a bulldog on a farm
A fish catching a man

I will put in the box
An adult turning into a baby
And a baby going back into a mother's stomach

My box is made
From every sweet in the world
With a gingerbread lid
Its locks are made of firing candy

I shall eat my box
All day
And it will never go away.

Adam Wiggins (10)
St Andrew's Primary School, Weymouth

THE MAGIC BOX

I will put in my box
Baby kittens and puppies crying
Roast potatoes crunching in my mouth
The juice of grapes

I will put in my box
The feel of puppies and kittens
The sight of foals walking
And the washing machine

I will put in my box
A tiger coming to school to learn
A grape crying like a baby
Strawberries carved in gravy

I will put in my box
A cat that barks like a dog
A dragon that miaows like a cat
An old lady winning a race

My box is made from seal fur
With crystals around
Its locks are glitter shells

I shall put a baby seal in it
And a sparkling of dust for wishes
And go to town
With Ms Espensen.

Stacey Mills (11)
St Andrew's Primary School, Weymouth

THE MAGIC BOX

I will put in my box
The smell of toffee and the taste of caramel
The touch of warm bath water
And electric, yellow, flash lightning

I will put in my box
The sight of fireworks
Crackling in the night
The sound of birds singing in the quiet

I will put in my box
Water coming out of a huge volcano
And a shark
Visiting the Sea Life Centre

I will put in my box
A bleating lion with white fur
And a roaring sheep
With a mane

My box is made from sparkling chandelier crystals
With a bronze key
Its locks are silver steel
Shining in the moonlight

I shall use my box
As a skate park
To ride in with my skateboard.

Joshua Betts (10)
St Andrew's Primary School, Weymouth

THE MAGIC BOX

I will put in my box
The bubbling of a witch's cauldron
The intoxicating fumes emitted from the hottest furnace
The taste of bitter air shrouded in mysterious gases

I will put in my box
The sleek fur of a cat shooting through my fingers
The bewildering spirits coming from the gloom
Screaming and ripping souls from everyone

I will put in my box
A man shaving his head
A hag with a sinister smile
A bull with a chicken's head

I will put in my box
A serpent with the head of a hound
And the wings of a bat
But also my sister's face grafted onto its behind

My box is made from
The skin of a snake
The key is made from cobwebs
And its locks from pure evil

I would go mad in my box
Run around screaming, relaxing
Jumping off the Empire State Building
(Of course I would become invincible first.)

Thomas Barnes (10)
St Andrew's Primary School, Weymouth

THE MAGIC BOX

I will put in the box
The song of a bumblebee
The smell of curry
The taste of melted ice cream

I will put in the box
The feel of ketchup on my tongue
The look of the long sea
The sight of a gold trophy

I will put in the box
The inside of a Dalek
The point of a pyramid
The sea of the dead

My box is made from
Liquorice and chocolate bars
With lumps of rock
Its locks are candy false teeth

I shall travel in my box
Through time and space
And put my room in it
Just like the Tardis.

Maxim Sorokopud (11)
St Andrew's Primary School, Weymouth

THE MAGIC BOX

I will put in my box
A shine of sparkly moonlight,
The sound of birds singing on a summer's morning,
The soft touch of a chestnut shell.

I will put in my box
A dazzling smile from a Hollywood star,
The sweet taste of mouth-watering strawberries,
The sight of sparkly grass on a frosty morning.

I will put in my box
A grant of three wishes from a magical genie,
The loss of a person who never lived,
The first word spoken by a tiny baby.

I will put in my box
A hiss from a lion and a roar from a snake,
A croak from a dog and a bark from a frog.

My box is fashioned from ice and crystal,
With jewels and stars on the lid,
Its hinges are the joints of my fingers.

I shall dive into my box and swim in its ocean,
Then me and my box
Will be washed up on a secret island.

Melissa Mahon (11)
St Andrew's Primary School, Weymouth

THE MAGIC BOX

I shall put in the box
The sound of peace and quiet and a cheeky dolphin laugh
The smell of pine wood just been cut
The taste of pizza and curry

I shall put in the box
The touch of slimy octopus and a smooth snake
The sun going down that is yellow and red
The sight of red, orange and yellow blazing fire

I shall put in the box
A slimy octopus sliding across the deck
A house full of bubbles
China dolls coming to life

I shall put in my box
A baby flying, a horse ice-skating
A person with a mouse's head
A lion that can speak

My box is made from
Gold, silver and metal
With patterns on the outside
Its locks are gold and diamonds

I shall get in the box
And slide down an icy hill.

Alice Bell (10)
St Andrew's Primary School, Weymouth

THE MAGIC BOX

I will put in the box
The roaring of stormy wind
The smell of petrol on a winter's day
The flavour of salt and vinegar crisps

I will put in the box
My dog's fur when it pricks up
As she runs to the front door
The mysterious grass on a windy day

I will put in the box
A dog with a human's head
A pencil case in an oven and chips in a pencil case
Snow in summer and heat in winter

I will put in my box
A fish with a hump and a camel with gills
Mr Meacham wetting himself
When we don't get our questions right

My box is made from ice
With a candyfloss key
Its locks are made from bears' teeth

I shall go in my box
And explore the Milky Way
Surf the highest tidal wave
And go hunting with a crossbow.

Aaron Sherlock (11)
St Andrew's Primary School, Weymouth

THE MAGIC BOX

I will put in my box

The sound of waves crashing against the rock
The smell of salty sea
The taste of sticky caramel

I will put in my box

The smoothness of birds' feathers
The small smile of a baby
Clouds racing along the sky

I will put in my box

The rubbery touch of a cow's nose
The quill of a porcupine
The flickering flames of fireworks

I will put in my box

A dog mooing and a cow barking
A scale on a camel and a hump on a fish
An oink of a horse and a neigh of a pig

My box is made from glistening crystal
With stars and moons on the top
Its key is gold and shiny

I shall read in it with a blanket
By stars in the lid that glow.

Stacey Green (10)
St Andrew's Primary School, Weymouth

Magic Box

I will put in my box,
The sound of the raindrops on the window
And the smell of silage put in the trailer
And the taste of cooked, hot sausages on the plate.

I will put in my box,
The two cold seasons,
Horses galloping through the fields
And the sight of newborn calves.

I will put in my box,
The smell of the farm
And the touch of a dog's tail,
The look of a cat's eyes.

I will put in my box,
The fur of the snake and the smoothness of the calf
And the long tail of a polar bear and the short tail of a dog,
The wing of a rhino and the horn of a bat.

My box is made from chestnut wood,
With a gold, funny key,
Its locks are like my little sister's face.

I shall dig a hole in a calf pen
And bury my box
And leave it until I'm 70,
Then dig it up.

Natalie Craig (11)
St Andrew's Primary School, Weymouth

THE MAGIC BOX

I will put in the box
The fearsome fangs of a fighting wolf,
The touch of a dragonfly's wing,
The stroke on a small dog's head.

I will put in the box
The ice cubes of a cool Coca-Cola,
The kind smile of a wrinkly grandparent,
The first blinding sunrise of a new year.

I will put in the box
The call of a Muslim priest,
The sweetness of baby turtles struggling out to sea,
The singing chant of an Irish pub.

I will put in the box
The power of a worm,
The cowardliness of a warrior,
The slowness of a cheetah.

My box is coated in fur, with poaches for pictures of family,
With gems on the top and smooth pebbles in the corners,
Its locks are made from glamorous purple stone.

I will run through beaches of polystyrene
And sleep on gigantic pebbles,
With pillows filled with dust from Heaven.

James Cole (11)
St Andrew's Primary School, Weymouth

MAGIC BOX

I will put in my box
The flick of a page being turned
The taste of homemade apple pie
A sparkle from a gleaming diamond

I will put in my box

The glint of a sparkling moon sailing through the sky
The purr of a cat curling up by the fire
The beauty of the white horses surfing into shore

I will put in my box

The first word of a child
Last breath of a person
The sweet sound of angels singing

I will put in my box

The sun at night and the moon all day
A witch on a bike
And a cyclist on a broomstick

My box shall be fashioned from gold
And covered by purple velvet and sparkling diamonds
The lid is the top of a hippo's mouth
With cobwebs in the corners, each holding their own story

In my box I shall gallop away into the sunset
And then finish
Surfing in the Caribbean with dolphins.

Cassie Hall (11)
St Andrew's Primary School, Weymouth

The Magic Box

I will put in my box

The purr of a cat
The fragrance of flowery perfume
The shine of stars on a moonlit night

I will put in my box

The soft touch of silk
The flowers swinging in the wind
The buzz of a bee

I will put in my box

A cat that sleeps all day
The loss of someone who never lived
And the first giggle from a baby

I will put in my box

A farmer on a boat
And a sailor on a tractor
A giggle from a lion
And a roar from a baby

My box is fashioned from jelly
On the top are sweets and cakes
The lock is made out of soft ice cream

I shall dance in my box
In the finest dress
I fly with the birds and talk to them.

Katie Dawling (11)
St Andrew's Primary School, Weymouth

THE MAGIC BOX

I will put in my box

The delicious smell of a cake being baked
The purr of a cat
The shine of the moon at night

I will put in my box

The song of a songbird as I wake up
The softness of a guinea pig's fur
The swish of a shooting star

I will put in my box

Three velvet wishes of a genie
The way a cat sleeps
The laugh of someone who never lived

I will put in my box

A farmer on a broomstick
And a witch in a tractor
A black moon and a silver sky

My box is fashioned from chocolate and gold
With diamonds on the lid and butterflies in the corners
The lock is fashioned from flowers

I shall flutter with
The butterflies until
I see lovely dolphins.

Catherine Burridge (11)
St Andrew's Primary School, Weymouth

THE MAGIC BOX

I will put in the box

The smooth touch of my mum at night
The heat of a blazing fire in winter
The softness of my bed in the morning

I will put in the box

The cold touch of a snowflake
The sound of sizzling bacon and sausages
The taste of jam coming out of a doughnut

I will put in my box

The sparkle in a dog's eyes
The word dentist in Gujarati
A good song by Elton John

I will put in my box

The hump of a dragon
The breath of fire of a snake
The acid spit of a hedgehog

My box is fashioned with bones
Holding the plates together,
The key and lock are made
Of a warthog skull

I will go down
Falling down, down, down,
To the underworld with it,
Floating in the pit
Of dead spirits.

Michael Whittle (10)
St Andrew's Primary School, Weymouth

THE MAGIC BOX

I will put in my box
The sweet smell on a summer's morning
The sight of a dog's beady eyes
A cat asleep on a sun-struck window sill
And a baby's first few cries

I will put in my box
The sun rising over a darkened hill
The song a siren sings
The bird's first take to the sky
And a flap of tiny wings

I will put in my box
Three humming words from a bee
A drop of sunlight though the moon is bright
Clouds forming like galloping horses
And a terrible, terrible fright

I will put in my box
A god on Earth like a mortal man
A polar bear waddling and a penguin roaring
A salad hot and a slab of meat cold
And a goalkeeper scoring

My box is made from crystal and gold
The keyhole is bright and shiny like the sun
The lid is like roof tiles
And the hinges are made of currant buns

I shall submerge in my box and see the sea life
I shall fly in my box and see the birds
I will go in my box and see the world
And I will hear the world's words.

Joseph Butcher (10)
St Andrew's Primary School, Weymouth

THE MAGIC BOX

I will put in my box
The squeal of a newborn puppy
A crunch of someone biting into some toast
The crackle of chips in a chip pan

I will put in my box
The sizzle of the bacon being made
And the smooth, silk nose of a horse
On a cold winter day

I will put in my box
A baby walking its first steps
The words of a lovely Irishman
The sight of the white horses crashing
Against the jagged rocks

I will put in my box
Eight seas and rain made of chocolate milkshake
A tiger purring and a cat roaring

My box will be fashioned with big, gold hinges
And silver plates
A grin on every corner of the box
And a big bright sun in the middle

I shall swim in my box
In the great seas with dolphins
And shall read all the books
In the world
Near a warm fire cuddled up to some dogs.

Harry McWilliams (11)
St Andrew's Primary School, Weymouth

THE MAGIC BOX

I would put in the box
The sound of the waves crashing against the rocks,
The sizzling sound of bacon,
The twinkle of a starry night.

I would put in the box
The smell of a scented flower,
The touch of a cat's wet fur,
The sound of a robin's call.

I would put in the box
A banana with pyjamas on,
Christmas decorations up in March,
A dog with no tail.

I would put in the box
A cat with six legs and a spider with four,
A princess with the face of an ogre
And an ogre with the face of a princess,
Sunshine in the night, moonlight in the day.

My box is fashioned from
A scale of a fish,
An eye of an eagle,
Gold and a block of ice,
The hooks would be made from ice cream and jelly.

I would surf in the box,
I would decorate my box,
I would live in the box!

Katherine Houston (10)
St Andrew's Primary School, Weymouth

THE MAGIC BOX

I will put in my box
The bark of a dog so excited
The song of a bird in the early morning
And the sweet scent of a restaurant in the distance

I will put in my box
A ball hitting the net and people roaring
The sight of flowers in the summer breeze
And the inside of a Creme Egg, so lush

I will put in my box
A pig riding a man
A worm chasing a bird
And a pot carrying a woman

I will put in my box
A baby giving birth to an adult
A snowman building a man
And a necklace wearing a woman

My box is made from gold, silver and bronze
With Zeus on top and Hades on the bottom
Its hinges are dinosaur bones

I shall race in my box
On the cobbled street
Of Saint Jean de Mont
And win every time.

James Davis (10)
St Andrew's Primary School, Weymouth

MY BOX!

I will put in the box
The sweet smell of a sponge baking in the oven,
The 'yummy in your tummy' taste of chocolate,
The laugh of my dad, loud and happy.

I will put in the box
The furry, fluffy feel of a cat's tummy,
The luscious smell of a sweet summer rose,
The feel of a daisy, soft and fresh.

I will put in the box
A sweet sparkle of a star on a silver swan,
A mermaid with a swishing tail,
The funny feel of a dolphin playing.

I will put in the box
A neigh of a dolphin, a creak of a horse, a croak of a cat,
A purr of a frog, *a spider* being scared of Ms Espensen!

My box is fashioned from pink and white roses,
With stars on the hinges
And horses on the top.

I will dance in my box on a beautiful stage,
With red velvet curtains, with magic behind them,
I will be clapped and cheered
And then I will disappear
Through the mysterious curtains.

Emily Hurst (10)
St Andrew's Primary School, Weymouth

The Magic Box

I will put in my box

The smell of a summer's night
Flush feathers of a hawk's wing
The tip of the bluest water touching a fingertip.

I will put in my box

The moon shining through a starry night sky
The touch of secrets flying by
The first laugh of a kitten purring

I will put in my box

The writing of a Chinese dragon
Printing Gujarati
A safari burning in the corner
The three wishes of a phoenix on a day's night

I will put in my box

The sparkle of a cobweb over the moon's light
A farmer on a red pony
And an Indian harvesting crops

My box is fashioned with silver petals and violet silk
The hinges are bronze with rust
I shall float in my box
Among the shadows
In the corners
Down in the Pacific.

Kelley Ireland (10)
St Andrew's Primary School, Weymouth

My Magic Box

I will put in my box

The shimmer of an angel high above,
The lively leap of a learning lion,
The sparkle of a starlit sky.

I will put in my box

The sound of a wave crashing motionless upon a shore,
The wonderful cover of a velvet book,
The miaow from a pussy cat's mouth.

I will put in my box

The glimmering tunnel of a rolling wave,
An eruption from a glowing volcano,
Snow falling gently on Christmas Day.

I will put in my box

A frozen beach and a boiling igloo,
A cuddly lion and ferocious teddy,
A green berry and a blue grape.

My box is fashioned from snowflakes and flowers,
The catches, from a lion,
The hinges. from a castle gate.

I shall swim with dolphins in my box
In the cool seas of the Atlantic Ocean,
I will then relax under the shade of a Caribbean palm tree
On a Caribbean beach.

Tamara Collier (11)
St Andrew's Primary School, Weymouth

THE MAGIC BOX

I would put in my box
The touch of silk inside a chestnut shell,
The lush smell of fresh cut grass,
The sound of crackling bacon.

I would put in my box
The sound of wings flapping high up in the sky,
The sparkle of an eye,
The lisp of someone speaking.

I would put in my box
The laughter of swaying trees,
Christmas Day in April,
A baby's first word.

I would put in my box
The squeal of a wolf, the howl of a mouse,
The scales of a cat, the fur of a dragon,
The blueness of a star, the sparkle of a mountain.

My box is fashioned from pure white fur, gold and a mother's kiss,
With glittering stars on the sides and wonderful jokes in the corners,
The hinges are like fingers clasping together.

I shall skate in my box gliding along the waters of Lake Placid,
Then I shall skate to a blazing hot desert
Where I shall stay in my dreams forever.

Jennifer Derrett (10)
St Andrew's Primary School, Weymouth

THE MAGIC BOX

I will put in the box
The sound of popping popcorn in the microwave
The crash of waves against the rocky rocks
And the wonderful taste of McDonald's chips

I will put in the box
The feel of my dog's velvety head
The sound of the lyrebirds' call
And the taste of caramel when creamy

I will put in the box
Gorgeous sugar that is healthy
A town of ever cleverness
And a boy with hair as long as Rapunzel's

I will put in the box
A centipede with 4 legs and a dog with 100
A girl with a howl of a voice and a wolf with the sweetest one on Earth
And a beach of diamonds and a mine of sand

My box is fashioned from fitted rubies
The key is from the Devil's horn
And the hinges are of old, gnarled bones

I will sunbathe in my box
On my beach of diamonds
And ride on the back of a dolphin into the sunset.

Charlotte Kaiser (10)
St Andrew's Primary School, Weymouth

THE MAGIC BOX

I will put in the box

The crackle of Coco Pops on a winter's morn,
The warm touch of a blazing fire,
The taste of chips straight out of the oven.

I will put in the box

The smell of fresh air in a field,
The feel of cat's soaked paws,
The sound of bacon sizzling in a pan.

I will put in my box

The sight of a dog walking a man,
The sight of a cat stroking a boy,
An ant squashing a car.

I will put in my box

The cry of a cat and the purr of an eagle,
The slice of an apple and the taste of a sword,
The squeal of a wolf and the howl of a pig.

My box is fashioned from

The finest chips money can buy,
The lid is made of the cheese in the moon,
The lock is made of the magic of a black mage's staff.

I will eat 100,000 chips in my box,
I will play the finest games in my box,
I will live happily in my box!

Daniel Houston (10)
St Andrew's Primary School, Weymouth

The Magic Box

I will put in my box

The final glimpse of the last sunset,
A swish of the Caribbean sea,
The tang of a strawberry touching the tip of my tongue.

I will put in my box

The wet smoothness of my dog's nose,
A tweet of an owl,
The first bark from my dog.

I will put in my box

The last smile from a friend,
The first crackle from a thunderstorm
And the first glimpse of a full moon.

I will put in my box

The four seasons,
A cowboy flying to the moon,
An astronaut on a brown horse.

My box is fashioned from gold and silver steel,
With diamonds in each corner,
Its hinges are the finger joints of an old man.

I shall run in my box all over the world,
I shall swim to the Caribbean
And land on a Barbados beach,
The colour of the golden sun.

Jemma Tewkesbury (11)
St Andrew's Primary School, Weymouth

THE MAGIC BOX

I will put in the box

The smooth touch of a resourceful rat's tail
The sizzling scent of frying mushrooms
The warmth of a mother's love

I will put in the box

The surprising sight of an old friend
The inspiring sound of music
The taste of a Chinese feast

I will put in the box

One thousand swords of the fallen brave
An afternoon with a lost loved one
The loyalty of a king's sovereign

I will put in the box

The light of night and the dark of day
A thirteen month and two hundred days
A friendly enemy and a nasty friend

My box is fashioned from books, finest
With lies in the corner, tucked away
It shall be inscribed with the flames of the sun

I shall read in my padded, soft box
The finest books of words
And I shall never have to sleep.

Hal Barker (11)
St Andrew's Primary School, Weymouth

THE MAGIC BOX

I will put in the box . . .

The sizzling scent of bacon frying,
The taste of sweet chocolate at Christmas,
The sight of the sun peering over the ocean.

I will put in the box . . .

The cold, cold touch of an icicle,
The boring words I hear from the teacher's mouth,
The soft silk inside a chestnut shell.

I will put in the box . . .

A loving memory of the deceased,
A thought of going to Heaven,
The first touch of a smooth, slithery snake.

I will put in the box . . .

A rider on a tractor and a farmer on a horse,
A silver sun and golden rain,
An astronaut as a teacher and a teacher in space.

My box is silver and gold,
With great big gems
And a padlock that's rusty and old.

I will swim with dolphins all day,
I would examine the ocean
And at night I would sleep under the stars and the moon.

Chloe Groves (10)
St Andrew's Primary School, Weymouth

THE MAGIC BOX

I will put in my box
A beautiful sizzling sunset,
A crumpled, crispy autumn leaf,
The sound of a red-breasted robin singing.

I will put in my box
The soft smoothness of snake's scales,
The roughness of an ancient dinosaur's skin,
The iciness of a freezing cold snowflake.

I will put in my box
A cat scaring a scary dog,
A hot camel swimming in the Atlantic sea,
Men and women with green, scaly skin.

I will put in my box
A devilish dog purring nicely,
A cat being taken for a long walk,
A huge butterfly roaring to itself.

My box is fashioned with a sunlight gold,
With fish scales on the shiny walls,
With ocean-deep sparkly pockets.

I will live in my box,
Dive into my ocean-deep pockets
And relax on a sandy beach,
Watching the sizzling sunset.

George Lane (11)
St Andrew's Primary School, Weymouth

The Magic Box

I will put in my box,
The sound of a snake hissing,
Ice from the whispery clouds,
The wonderful swish on a moonlit night.

I will put in my box,
The claw of an ancient dinosaur,
A touch of the wind that crosses your face,
The three wishes of a phoenix's tail.

I will put in my box,
The sound of two swords meeting,
The twang from an archer's bow
And the smash of a mace on a shield.

I will put in my box,
The sixth season and a golden moon,
A fish with a rod
And a fisherman in the sea.

My box is fashioned from ice and gold,
The key is made from a hippogriff's beak,
The hinges are made from beaten copper.

My box will uncover secrets
That should never be told
And unleash the forces of chaos.

Maxwell Vallance (10)
St Andrew's Primary School, Weymouth

The Magic Box

I will put in my box
The crunch of icy snow
The dew of the morning grass
The sound of a pebble hitting the water

I will put in my box
The whispering of an icy wind
The feeling of rain touching my face
And the shimmering sun shining on the waves

I will put in my box
Ten eyes of a five-headed dog
The sight of Max with five ears and two noses
And the sight of a phoenix's tear

I will put in my box
A snowman in a desert, camel in the North Pole
Sun at night
And moon at day

My box is fashioned with glass, gold and silver
The key is made out of an elephant's tusk
The hinges are made of the jaw of an sabre-toothed tiger

I will fly in my box
And lie on soft, golden sand
And I shall sunbathe.

Tommy Jones (10)
St Andrew's Primary School, Weymouth

MONSTER REPTILE

D ragon-shaped monster,
I ndagoan have very blunt teeth,
N o dinosaurs had any hair,
O n ice, easily break through,
S o never teach one to skate
A nd never bring one to school,
U nderwater dinosaurs swim a lot,
R aging through the sea.

Luke Davis (8)
St Andrew's Primary School, Weymouth

FRIENDS

F riends are kind, caring and helpful,
R unning around is what we like to do,
I like all my friends,
E very day we play together,
N one of them are unkind to me,
D aytime is my favourite time to play with my friends,
S ome of my friends are really cool.

Danielle Luke (8)
St Andrew's Primary School, Weymouth

THE BIRD

It sings a happy song sitting in the tree
Feathers as soft as a blanket
It looks like an aeroplane with wings outstretched
It gets scared by cars
And looks like a kite in the sky
It is called back by its mum.

Karl Newton (9)
St George's School, Bourton

THE LONELY OAK

An old oak stands in the corner of the playground,
Ignored.
Its old, wrinkled arms reaching out as if to catch affection.
Lonely.
Scars all over its body from being hacked at.
Stripped bare - no life.
A sad, lonely, old man.
In front light - behind, darkness.
Roots crawling about the old man.
Tangling feet.
Poor, weather-beaten, crinkly, old oak,
Only wants affection.
I feel sorry for this poor, weary, gnarled, wrinkly,
Ancient, old oak that stands in the corner of the playground.

Naomi Samuelson (9)
St George's School, Bourton

MY FRIEND, THE SUN

The brightest star in the midnight sky,
Shining like an untouched pearl.
It bellows heat to all the world,
Even the poorest slave,
Even the youngest child.
It lights up unhappy faces,
It comforts people in the dark and cold.

The sun is a happy, gentle person who warms your heart
And touches your soul.
Her radiant streaks blind the eye,
Her happy smile is bigger than you.

Harriet Walker (10)
St George's School, Bourton

NIGHT SKY

The day has gone,
The night is here,
No children playing,
No birds singing,
All is silent, darkness covers the sky,
Everyone tucked into their beds . . .
Suddenly!
A thunderbolt falls from the sky, the land trembles with fear,
Then the lightning strikes back as quick as a flash,
Striking the lonely tree.
Thankfully it stops,
The moon comes out from its hiding place,
The stars come to play, shining like fairy lights,
Covering the sky,
The moon a lantern, lighting the sky,
Forever!

Olivia Worthington (9)
St George's School, Bourton

WHITE FLUFFY CLOUDS

Different shapes in the sky,
Some funny, some sad.
Most move, people say it's the sea sucking them in.
People say they're pretty cute,
Others say they tell a story,
Even more say they remind them of a moment of their life.

Scientists believe they protect us,
Others believe they represent something.
Sometimes they're bad,
Sometimes they're good.

Oliver Swan (11)
St George's School, Bourton

THE TREE WHO BLESSED THE WINTER

I am old, stripped bare and cold
The autumn has stolen my coat
That I'm using to cover my floor.
I want a child to sit in my branches, to warm me.
No one comes, I reach out my branches,
I look like an old, wrinkled man.

I stare at the evergreens,
Longing for their leaves.
Soon the winter comes,
I am cold and start to shiver.
But the winter is not all bad!

Soon a new white coat falls from the sky,
I reach out my branches and catch it,
As it comes down, I am filled with glory.
I am now a beautiful marvel for everyone to stare at,
In my wonderful, new, white coat,
Now I am warm and cosy, I love the winter.

Lottie Lobb (9)
St George's School, Bourton

SWIMMING

S   wimming up and down
W idths and lengths
I   n the pool
M oving all about
M um and Dad cheering me on
I   n butterfly, backstroke, breaststroke, freestyle
N early ready, cozzie on
G oggles on, go, go, gone.

Maddy Hollick (9)
St George's School, Bourton

RAIN

It's raining, it's pouring,
It's all very boring,
We can't go out to play,
What shall we do today?

It's raining, it's pouring,
It's all very boring,
Everybody is snoring,
We'll just sit inside
And wish we were at the seaside.

Hooray, hooray, the rain stopped today,
Now we can go out to play,
We know what to do today!

Tom Barton (8)
St George's School, Bourton

THE BIRD

Singing in the trees,
Hidden from sight,
Flying past to say hello,
Singing happy songs,
His feathers as soft as silk,
Playing catching games
And then he's on his way again,
Frightened by cars and off
With his wings outspread,
Like an eagle's wings,
Up, up and away,
Bye-bye bird!

Lian Willow Denyer (9)
St George's School, Bourton

THE TREE

I love company from others, loving care they give me,
Some of my branches are very thin and delicate,
The rain is nice, it gives me a drink,
I love to get wet, but I hate getting soggy,
I'm very tall, wrinkly and old,
I'm rough, as in my skin,
Some of my branches are very thick but nice,
I could never be a waste of space,
I'm always trying to make new friends,
I'm dark brown, light brown and green in places,
I'm tall, proud and reaching out,
I love to play tag with children,
But I hate my branches being pulled off
And my body being kicked,
I hate to be stripped naked because I get very cold,
I am very bendy and straight,
I love to be touched,
Some people just take no notice of me,
As if I'm a helpless old tree.

Natalie Birley (10)
St George's School, Bourton

THE TREE

Big hands that can reach anywhere,
A wrinkly tree with rotting bark.
Branches like an old man's hand,
Every year the autumn strips him bare.

The winter is cold,
The fingertips of the tree freeze,
He screams in the wind,
He tries to move his branches, but he can't, they are frozen.

At last it's spring, it has been a long winter,
He feels his bark getting warmer,
He puts a little smile on his face,
He's glad it's warm again.

The summer is hot,
He wants to be cold again,
The sun is beating down on him,
He is getting sunburnt on his old bark,
He feels like he's going to die.

Sam Bingham (10)
St George's School, Bourton

IT'S NOT FAIR!

It's not fair . . .
    because my friends pushed me.

It's not fair . . .
    because my friend got an ice cream.

It's not fair . . .
    because my friend slammed the door on me.

It's not fair . . .
    because my friend ruined the display and blamed it on me.

It's not fair . . .
    because my friend stole my work.

It's not fair . . .
    because my friend said I'm stupid.

It is fair . . .
    because my friend has lost his play time!

Daniel Turner (8)
St George's School, Bourton

I Want My Teddy Back!

Mum's took my teddy
I don't know what to do!
I'll rip up the sofa
I'll smash the glasses and all the pottery
I'll go on hunger strike
I'll rampage around
Smashing everything in front of me
I'll hate my mum for taking my teddy
I'll lock myself in the cupboard
I won't go to bed
I'll make lots of noise
In the end I didn't do any of these things
In the end I was good
And Mum gave me my teddy back.

Jake McClung (9)
St George's School, Bourton

Just Like . . .

Trees are green
They like to be seen
Just like my jeans in the washing machine

Bears are brown
They like to dance up and down
Just like the zip on my dressing gown

Stars are white
They shine very bright
Just like the lights on my motorbike.

Tasmin Hunt (8)
St George's School, Bourton

HEY STEVE

'Hey Steve, did you like that history lesson?'
'Boring!'
'But we did research.'
'Boring!'
'But Christopher Columbus is cool.'
'No, he is not.'
'What about the ruler fight?'
'Now that was cool!'

'Hey Steve, did you like that art lesson?'
'Boring!'
'Did you like my drawing?'
'No!'
'But Picasso's cool.'
'No, he is not.'
'Did you like that chalk fight?'
'Now that was cool!'

'Hey Steve, did you like that geography lesson?'
'Boring!'
'What, you didn't like the experiment?'
'Boring!'
'What about the protractor fight?'
'Now that was cool.'

'Hey Steve, did you like that maths lesson?'
'Boring!'
'But we did multiplication.'
'Boring!'
'But the Gelosia method is cool.'
'No, it is not!'
'But the pencil fight was cool.'
'Now that was cool!'

Garreth Ball (10)
St George's School, Bourton

THE SEA

Buried treasure in the sea
Buried treasure just for me
Fishes swimming in and out
Whales spraying with their spout
Dolphins squeaking and eating fish
Dolphins love this tasty dish
Sharks killing and pulling apart
Eating the body and eating the heart
Slimy seaweed tangles you up
And seals swim with their baby pup
At the bottom, bones rot
And eels swim with their electric shot
Walruses flop with their tusks up high
Pointing right up into the sky
Crabs click and move sideways
To them the sea is like a maze
Slippery water snakes slither through
Watch out that they don't bite you!

Amelia Mobsby (9)
St George's School, Bourton

FIREWORK NIGHT

Firework night sometimes gives me a fright
When the fireworks go bang
And the beautiful sparkles
Wake me from my bed

I look out of my window
And see the lovely, colourful lights
In the sky
And then I think of what lovely things
Fireworks are . . .

Gemma Martin (9)
St George's School, Bourton

SAFETY

This is my poem about safety,
You should never be too hasty.

Always say 'No' to a stranger,
You could be in danger.

Don't play with matches
Or you will end up in ashes.

Don't put water on a chip pan fire,
If you do, it will get even higher.

Don't play in the kitchen
Or your fingers will be missin'.

You should get a smoke detector,
It could be your life protector.

You want to be safe in every way,
That's all I can really say.

Hannah Plowman (8)
St George's School, Bourton

MY DOG

My dog is very funny,
My dog is very skinny,
My dog does all kinds of things.

My dog sits,
My dog does tricks,
My dog wolfs down food,
My dog laps water up.

My dog can be very cheeky,
But my dog can be very sweet.

I love my dog!

Jenny Valentine (9)
St George's School, Bourton

THE SKY

My breath is gentle
It blows on everyone,
My sheep sometimes cry
As well as make ice
But they are lovely, floating things,
I like to play marbles
But they drop on everyone,
But my best thing of all,
My pride and joy
The sun that will never die.

Thomas Kingscott (11)
St George's School, Bourton

THE TREE

The tree is as mouldy as an old fruit
Like lots of rockets taking off
Looks like an old spider
But the tree is an old man
The tree is as solid as a rock
It is like a big monster trying to grab you
Its branches are scarred
From battles it has fought
But it stands still
Watching the people
Waiting for the summer.

Ben Hunt (9)
St George's School, Bourton

THE TREE

Old and rotten skeleton
Withered, old fingers, knobbly knees
Old and bent fingers, stripped and bare
Arms reaching out for company
Sucking in old age and the knowledge of people long dead
Texture rough and ancient
Scars where arms and legs have been amputated
Creaking and groaning, all it can do is stand there
And watch the world pass by
Just an old and rotten skeleton.

Saoirse Koch (9)
St George's School, Bourton

WHEN YOU ARE A BABY

I want my mummy, mummy
I am very hungry, hungry
It's not very funny, funny
When you are a baby

She has my dummy, dummy
I am very hungry, hungry
It's not very funny, funny
When you are a baby

I want my daddy, daddy
I am very hungry, hungry
It's not very funny, funny
When you are a baby.

Stefan Brown (11)
St Joseph's RC Combined School, Poole

DOLPHIN

She swims in her big roomful cove,
Where her pods are resting with love,
She snatches her prey like a wolf catching a dove.

She's not as kind as you think,
She does not make you wink,
Did you know whales and dolphins
Are relatively linked?

Victoria Lawlor (9)
St Joseph's RC Combined School, Poole

TUTANKHAMUN

There was a tomb in a far away land
All the treasure waiting to be found
Under the shiny sand
Henry Carter and a camel climbed over the mound
To the deserted land
Looking for artefacts
Henry started to dig through the sand

He found ten steps going down
Slowly he stepped down
And opened the great find
For he had found Tutankhamun
And the hidden treasure.

Georgina McLaughlin (11)
St Joseph's RC Combined School, Poole

SWEETHEART

Sweetheart, my sweetheart, how I love you
When I sit on a bench, I think about you
I write in my files about you
I wish I could kiss you for a little while
I lay in my bed and dream about you
I wish I could see you
I love you
And my dream has come *true*.

Emily Fisk (8)
St Joseph's RC Combined School, Poole

POP STARS

Pop stars are famous
Pop stars are great
Pop stars like singing
And staying up late

Pop stars are lucky
And good at dancing too
Pop stars miss their families
And are always waiting for their cue

So that's about pop stars
Maybe it's about you
I want to be one
I hope you do too.

Lydia Gibbons (9)
St Joseph's RC Combined School, Poole

THE NUTS

I'm looking for my treasure,
I hid it very good.
I know it's in a tree somewhere,
So come on, let's see.
Along the leafy ground go,
Up a tree to see what I found.
Oh no! Oh dear! My lovely nuts have disappeared.
I know I'll look in every tree,
I will not ever find my precious nuts.
I'm going to check this tree,
Oh loo, I found them, yippee!

John Adkins (10)
St Joseph's RC Combined School, Poole

HIDDEN TREASURE

In the desert,
Really, really hot,
Find the treasure.
Fake the lot.
Dig and dig
With all your might,
Find the entrance
With your light.
Pull and pull,
Until you die,
Search the tombs,
With fate and fear.
Open the door
And see the rich expenses
Of the past.
Now we find the tomb
Of the king who rests
In peace forever more,
Until woken again.

Claire Frigot (11)
St Joseph's RC Combined School, Poole

THE TIGER

Inside the tiger's heart lives the flames
Inside the flames lies his courage
Inside his courage is his freedom
Inside his freedom is the cry of a human
Inside the cry of a human lies love beneath
Inside the love beneath is his mother
Inside his mother is the tiger's heart.

Jade Cadby (9)
St Joseph's RC Combined School, Poole

THIS IS THE MOUTH

This is the mouth
that ate the lunch
and drank lemonade,
yesterday made.

This is the mouth
that burped and burped,
shattering the class,
breaking the glass.

This is the mouth
that would not shut up,
talking about something
I don't care about.

This is the mouth
that spat on the cat,
spitting and spitting
and said 'Take that!'

This is the mouth
that ate the lunch,
that burped and burped,
that would not shut up,
that spat on the cat.
This is the mouth
and that's that!

Brendan Byrne (9)
St Joseph's RC Combined School, Poole

A GOLDEN MORNING

Yellow the bracken
Golden the sheaves
Rosy the apples
Crimson the leaves

When leaves are falling
My friends are calling
The glass windows are covered
With a golden awning.

Elizabeth Martin (10)
St Joseph's RC Combined School, Poole

TREASURE

Where will I find it?
Under the sea?
In the tallest tower
Or even in a hotel?

I'll check from top to bottom
In every place I can think of
But still nothing.

I won't stop searching for it
For I'm a Scottish man
When I find this treasure . . .

I tripped over something
It wasn't very nice
I went bump, ouch, bump, ouch!

I looked at the large object,
I said, 'Yabba-dabba-doo,
I found it!'

I smashed it open with a hammer
In delight, the door creaked.

I had a gleaming smile
In there were 15,000 diamonds
And a red ruby.

Ben Absolom (11)
St Joseph's RC Combined School, Poole

THE DOG'S BONE

I got a bone.
What shall I do with it?
I will bury it,
I will chew it,
I will bite it.

Dig it up again
And again and again.
Pull it out!
It's dirty,
It's smelly.

I bark and bark,
I play with the bone,
I wrestle with the bone,
I growl at the bone,
I will bury it again.

Benito Viola (10)
St Joseph's RC Combined School, Poole

THINK OF A DRINK

For a hidden treasure you have to think,
In your mind you think of drink.
Will it be Guinness for those who wait?
No, that will leave you in an awful state.
Will it be Heineken for those who smile?
Actually that might take a while.
What about whisky, dark and strong?
But that oft' gives off a pong.
Whatever you decide to drink,
Trust me, it won't help you think.

Anthony Matthews (10)
St Joseph's RC Combined School, Poole

BURIED TREASURE

I'm running very fast,
through the open grass,
dodging all the trees,
hovered with a breeze.

I jump over walls,
kick the footballs,
ducking under washing lines,
the smell of apple pies.

I can smell it now,
getting much closer,
finally I dig
for my treasure.

I run back home,
to chew my treasure,
I lay in my kennel
and have a long nap.

Michael Godden (10)
St Joseph's RC Combined School, Poole

TORNADO

Church-masher
Building-smasher
House-twirler
People-whirler
Bottom-nipper
Shorts-ripper
Sky-rider
Air-glider.

Domenico Salvia (9)
St Joseph's RC Combined School, Poole

THE GOLDEN PLATE

I ran outside as I saw
A shiny thing in the garden
I ran up to it
The shiny, golden thing
It was a golden plate
There were drawings of a map
I was surprised to find this golden plate
I folded the map
It leads me to a ship
I got on
Then it started to move
I was scared a little bit until it stopped
It was murky in the water
But I could just see a chest . . .

James Tucker (10)
St Joseph's RC Combined School, Poole

THE EAGLE'S EYE

Inside the eagle's eye, a burning sun.
Inside the burning sun, the eagle's beak.
Inside the eagle's beak, the jagged rocks.
Inside the jagged rocks, the eagle's feathers.
Inside the eagle's feathers, the enormous plunges.
Inside the enormous plunges, the eagle's claw.
Inside the eagle's claw, the dehydrated ground.
Inside the dehydrated ground, the eagle's wings.
Inside the eagle's wings, the dead trees.
Inside the dead trees, the eagle's eye.

Ryan Trowbridge (9)
St Joseph's RC Combined School, Poole

THE MANSION

The mansion, creepy ghouls,
Restless spirits inside,
You won't believe
What's inside the creepy mansion,
Creepy ghouls, restless spirits,
You won't believe what's
Inside.

Ashley Dunford (8)
St Joseph's RC Combined School, Poole

FRIENDS

Friends are great
Friends are fun
Friends shine bright
Just like the sun.

Sophie Angell (9)
St Joseph's RC Combined School, Poole

THE MONKEY

Gripping branches, tree to tree
Always likes to feel free
Screaming and bellowing awfully.

Max Forward (10)
St Joseph's RC Combined School, Poole

WINTER

W inter is here
I cy ponds
N umb toes
T oo cold to play out
E ver so cold
R ake up the leaves.

Freya Gill (8)
St Joseph's RC Combined School, Poole

FLUFFY

My dog named Fluffy
Is white and scruffy
And is always jumping around
He never sits still
Until I will
He's the best dog around.

Mariette Trott (9)
St Joseph's RC Combined School, Poole

MY TORTOISE

My tortoise moving slowly across the soft green grass,
Looking in every hedge, picking up all the glass,
My tortoise running across the road
And on his back is a big, heavy load!

Aine Wood (9)
St Joseph's RC Combined School, Poole

CRYSTAL

Inside the gofer's burrow, the vast land.
Inside the vast land, the gofer's fur.
Inside the gofer's fur, the lonely tree.
Inside the lonely tree, the gofer's ear.
Inside the gofer's ear, the only weed.
Inside the only weed, the gofer's burrow.

Lewis Connor (9)
St Joseph's RC Combined School, Poole

DOLPHINS

Dolphins are lovely,
Dolphins are rare,
Slippery and blue.
When they dive in the water
And out again,
The water will splash you!

Megan Davis (10)
St Joseph's RC Combined School, Poole

THERE'S A ...

There's a sticky micky spider
There's a drunk munk spider
There's a silly billy spider
There's a willing and not willing spider
There's a mighty spider.

David Rudenko (8)
St Joseph's RC Combined School, Poole

HIDDEN TREASURES

There somewhere in
the deep blue sea

Somewhere no one
can find them

Only the sea animals
know where they are

Do you know
what I am talking about?

Of course you do

Hidden treasures!

Charlotte Clarke (10)
St Michael's CE Primary School, Bournemouth

THE SNAIL

Once there was a little snail,
Whose shell was as big as his tail.
His slimy body leaves a trail on the ground,
He is so small, he doesn't make a sound.

His eyes stick out of his head,
To look for his food, so he is fed.
For food he eats leaves
And snails never get fleas!

Snails are very slimy,
They are also gooey and grimy.
Munching leaves all day long,
When they've eaten, everything's gone!

Charlotte Marshall (9)
St Michael's CE Primary School, Bournemouth

THE MAGICAL LAVENDER

There was once a unicorn,
Whose name was Lavender.
She galloped gracefully,
Across the crystal waters.
Her mane flowed back,
With so much beauty.
Lavender was so intelligent,
So magical.
She galloped with so much freedom,
Speed and harmony.
Her horn glistened,
When the sun shone on her.
Lavender had so much wisdom,
She was simply beautiful.

Alice Chatfield (10)
St Michael's CE Primary School, Bournemouth

MY GOLDFISH

I have a pet tiger,
He is called Mr McGuire,
My goldfish ate it,
It meant to shake it.
My pet lion started to roar,
But now it's dead on the floor,
Now my goldfish has eaten an elephant,
That used to be quite elegant.
My goldfish has now eaten a stampede of bulls,
You never know, he might eat some seagulls.
Sometimes I wish my goldfish would eat my sister!
But then I would probably miss her.

Alice Ivory (10)
St Michael's CE Primary School, Bournemouth

ANIMALS

A
 bear,
  a
   bear
    has
     caught
      the
       mayor.

Monkey,
 monkey
  up
   a
    tree,
     look,
      there's
       a
        bee.

The
 cat,
  the
   cat
    has
     eaten
      a
       rat,
        quick
         before
          he
           gets
            my
             mat.

Tiger,
 tiger
  on
   the
    floor,
   get
    up
     it's
      your
       turn
      to
       roar.

Chenice Manning (10)
St Michael's CE Primary School, Bournemouth

L DORA

My name is Laura, my friends called me L Dora
And I'm waiting outside the hospital.
You see - I'm only six,
I feel all in a mix.
My mum's having a baby,
I think it will drive me crazy.
Mum gave me a lolly
To say she was sorry
That she wouldn't be there
To take me to the fair.
Today I screamed and cried all day long,
To try to cheer me up, Dad sang me a song.
We're at the hospital, me and my dad,
Waiting for the baby to come - I feel quite glad.
They should be out quite soon, quite fast,
Here they are - at last!

Kate Dawson (9)
St Michael's CE Primary School, Bournemouth

HIDDEN TREASURES

In a faraway land of bare grass,
There lived a little squirrel named Eric.
In his cosy tunnelled nest with shiny glass,
Surrounding his entire small home.

He rapidly scurried around in a field,
Looking longingly for a giant shiny ring.
Eric had not yet found it,
But he still ran on, as the birds started to sing.

He suddenly came across something silver,
Eric ran quickly and saw it glistening in the sun.
The puzzled squirrel picked it up and sniffed
And ran back looking like he had had fun.

Eric lived happily with his shiny collection,
But every day Eric used to measure
His glistening silver and gold collection,
Which he called, Eric's hidden treasure.

Jodie Lydia Radulovitch (10)
St Michael's CE Primary School, Bournemouth

HIDDEN TREASURES

F   ootball
O   ffside
O   wn goal
T   urf
B   oots
A   way match
L   inesman
L   eague.

Michael Goodrich (10)
St Michael's CE Primary School, Bournemouth

The Mystery Of The Black Thing

I slowly crept down the stairs
As other people call it apples and pears
And then I saw it, it was greyish-black
So I turned around to run straight back.

It started to chase me, then kill me I thought
But I turned back and I even fought
It suddenly threw me to the floor
But I could not fight, no, not any more.

It stared at me so I stared at it too
And then I asked it, 'Who are you?'
It answered me in a low, deep voice
'I am . . .' *Bang!* there was a loud noise.

'What was that?' I cried 'it must be bad!'
'Don't worry, it was only me,' said Dad
Oh no, Dad's awake, what now? What shall I do?
I turned to the thing, it wasn't there, now it's out to get . . . *you!*

Taranjeet Lall (10)
St Michael's CE Primary School, Bournemouth

Untitled

There's a rhino at the zoo
It's coming to get you
You wouldn't have a clue
His horns are bug
His face is scary
So do please be very wary
Nothing about him is small
His skin is as thick as a wall.

Arabella Da Costa (9)
St Michael's CE Primary School, Bournemouth

CANDY LAND

When I was twelve, I had a dream,
Of strawberries and ice cream,
Chocolates, sweets, slides and swings,
But they were not all that they seemed.

For everything was made of sugar,
The sweets, the slides and even the burgers.

It was such a lovely place,
I wish I could take it home in a case,
I made the most of it while I could,
Before my alarm clock went and then I should
Get up, shower and then get dressed,
I hope I have this dream again - it was the *best!*

Grace Nevill (10)
St Michael's CE Primary School, Bournemouth

TREES

Trees, trees, as tall as the sky
Trees, trees, they are really high

Trees, trees, they have a thousand leaves
Trees, trees, they don't have any teeth

Trees, trees, they have brown bark
Trees, trees, they perform really good art

Trees, trees, they blow and blow around
Trees, trees, their trunks are really round.

Craig Hancock (9)
St Michael's CE Primary School, Bournemouth

SCARY THINGS

I hate the dark,
It's the perfect time for creatures to lark,
Ghosts and ghouls
Are worse than schools.
Knights and dragons,
Witches in wagons.
Vampires are the living dead,
Insects crawling around under my bed!

Some people faint at the sight of blood,
Others when it's stormy are frightened of a flood.
Some creatures are just imagination,
But others come from the world's creation!

Katya Rose (10)
St Michael's CE Primary School, Bournemouth

FERRARI

F   ast and furious they race down the road.
E   agerly rushing to the finishing line.
R   ed or yellow, sometimes black, shining on the sunlit track.
R   evving their engines until they're hot.
A   lmost like a rocket.
R   eaching the chequered flag.
I   want one!

Ross Welsh (9)
St Michael's CE Primary School, Bournemouth

Hidden Treasure

I love my mum
She's cuddly and sweet
She's loves me a lot
She buys things to eat

I like my dad
He's fit and he's cool
He cooks me my tea
He can be quite a fool

I hate my brother
He bullies me bad
He is so crazy
He thinks I'm lazy

I hate my sister
She steals all my things
She stole all my make-up
She stole my best ring

I love Milly
She's furry and fat
She sleeps all day long
She's my special cat.

Yolanda Jacob (9)
St Michael's CE Primary School, Bournemouth

What's Winter?

Winter is freezing cold,
The people snuggle up as the old.
Skiing down the steepest hill,
You don't have to pay the bill.

Going out into the snow,
Will you have to do a show?
Go and put on your gloves,
As your friend shoves.

Sandra Pita (10)
St Michael's CE Primary School, Bournemouth

MY WONDERFUL DAYDREAM

I want to be a pirate
And look for silver and gold.
I want my own pirate ship,
To sail across the sea.

I want to be a footballer
And listen to the roar of the crowd.
I want to tackle and get the ball,
To score a *brilliant* goal.

I want to be a scuba-diver
And swim underneath the sea.
I want to look at all the beautiful fish,
To see how deep they swim.

I want to be a pop star
And sing in concerts, live.
I want to stand in front of a crowd,
To sing extremely *loud!*

But at the end of the day, I'm just me,
In a wonderful daydream.

Lucy Jones (9)
St Michael's CE Primary School, Bournemouth

SEASONS

When I go for a walk in the spring,
The birds sing,
Lambs are born
And daffodils blossom.

When I go for a walk in the summer,
The sun shines
In the blue skies,
As children eat their ice creams.

When I go for a walk in the autumn,
The wind blows
And leaves turn gold,
As it joins winter and summer together.

When I go for a walk in the winter,
It's cold and icy,
As snow goes on the bare trees
And the dark nights seem to never end.

Holly Nicholson (10)
St Michael's CE Primary School, Bournemouth

SNAKES

Snakes are scaly and slithering,
Snakes are wormy and wriggly,
Snakes squirm and squiggle,
Through leaves and grasses.
Snakes hiss with their thin tongues,
Snakes bite with their strong fangs,
Snakes have sharp, piercing eyes.

Andrew Mason (9)
St Michael's CE Primary School, Bournemouth

ALPHABET

A utumn wind
B irds that sing
C olourful leaves
D awn breaks through the trees
E ntertaining guests
F rightening tests
G rateful people
H igh church steeples
I guanas lying down
J umping on the ground
K icking kids
L emonade lids
M aking cakes and
N ewly-cooked steaks
O pen doors
P attering floors
Q uarrelling children
R unning outdoors
S tarlight
T wilight
U rban leaves
V anishing trees
W afting breeze
X -ray eyes
Y outh that flies
Z zzzzz.

Jemma Derby (9)
St Michael's CE Primary School, Bournemouth

THE GIRL WHO DIDN'T KNOW WHAT TO WRITE

She could not think,
her brain was bare.
Her face went pink,
she did not care.

She pulled her hair,
began to blink.
It was not fair,
she could not think.

What could she write
That would impress,
The teacher who
was in distress?

If only she could
see the light.
To think it through,
to get it right.

Then suddenly,
it was clear.
She had found
a great idea.

Right in her lap,
a poem lay.
Complete and finished,
in every way!

Nina Luminati (10)
St Michael's CE Primary School, Bournemouth

MY SECRET TREASURE

I have a treasure
But it's a secret

> I talk to Him
> I laugh with Him

I dine with Him
He's my best friend

> He's in my heart
> He's in my soul

He's in my house
He's in my family

> If I'm lonely
> I remember He's with me

If I'm sad
I know He's there

> I remember He's with me
> Because He died for me

He's my treasure
He gave me life

> He's my friend
> My secret

He's my hidden treasure
He's my loving God.

Emma Jones (9)
St Thomas Garnet's School, Bournemouth

HIDDEN TREASURE

I have a hidden treasure
I have friends
I have a roof over my head
I have God who looks after me

I have a hidden treasure
I have friends
I can write and draw
I have a roof over my head
I have an education

I have a hidden treasure
It is . . .
I have love and care.

Rachel Gillings (9)
St Thomas Garnet's School, Bournemouth

HIDDEN TREASURE

This is my secret
My parents and me
Oh what a wonder for you to see
My mum and dad together
Made me
That is my secret you see

They are my hidden treasure
My mum and my dad
They are the best treasure
I've ever had.

Natalie Wedge (9)
St Thomas Garnet's School, Bournemouth

HIDDEN TREASURE

Hidden treasure
Lots of pleasure
Not just gold
Not just riches

Hidden treasure
I am lucky that I
Do maths and measure
My education
Not just sensation

My hidden treasure
Is love, it comes
From my parents
Like it came from above
My hidden treasure.

Peter Landi (9)
St Thomas Garnet's School, Bournemouth

AUSTRALIAN CHRISTMAS

It really was a very strange way,
The way I spent last Christmas Day.

Instead of it being cold and wet,
In Western Australia I did sweat.

The sun was bright,
The sea was blue.

The surf was white,
A fantastic view.

Todd Lewis (10)
St Thomas Garnet's School, Bournemouth

DEEP BELOW THE OCEAN

Deep below the ocean,
Where the witches live,
Where they play with potions,
You can hear them saying, 'Give.'

Deep below the ocean,
Where the creatures lie,
In a soft motion,
You see them die and die.

Deep below the ocean,
Where the sunblock is,
Where the people rub their lotion,
You can still hear the fizz.

Deep below the sea,
Is where I am free,
I have lots of fun,
Even though there is no sun!
I am Maria the mermaid.

Rayna Chauhan (10)
St Thomas Garnet's School, Bournemouth

HIDDEN TREASURE

I have a gift,
I call it my hidden treasure.
I can taste a cake
And swim in a lake.

I have a gift,
I call it my hidden treasure.
I have a house,
Yes, complete with a mouse.

I have a gift,
I call it my hidden treasure.
I have a brain to know where I'm going,
I can see when it's been snowing.

I have a gift,
I call it my hidden treasure.
I can see the flowers that grow in May,
I have someone with whom to play.
Yes, that is my gift!

Kimberley Sobisch (10)
St Thomas Garnet's School, Bournemouth

NATURE! NATURE!

Nature is in our homes,
Nature is in our towns,
Nature is in our forests, it's all around.

Nature is blue,
Nature is green,
The colours of the rainbow are
Shining on me.

Animals are running,
Birds are singing,
Fish are wriggling,
Nature is alive and growing.

Rivers are flowing,
Trees are waving
And the rain is still pouring.

Louis Luke (7)
St Thomas Garnet's School, Bournemouth

Hidden Treasures

I have hidden treasures,
I am so rich, not poor.
But not with silver or gold
Or possessions you can hold.

I can eat more and more,
Buy anything in a store.
I could live until I'm old,
Unlike Africans who are cold.

I have a family and a home,
I'm getting lots of education.
I can eat treats like a triple chocolate cone,
To poor people that's just imagination.

Oliver Porter (10)
St Thomas Garnet's School, Bournemouth

My Saxophone

My sax is big and gold,
It's rather heavy to hold.
It has lots of keys to press,
Over twenty-three no less.

The sound annoys my bigger brother,
But not my sister nor my mother.
My dad sometimes puts up with it,
But only for a little bit.

I think my sax is really cool
And so do all my friends at school.
They love to hear me when I play,
So I think I'll join a band one day.

Jennifer Law (10)
St Thomas Garnet's School, Bournemouth

HIDDEN TREASURE

I have hidden treasure
And if I wrote it down and measured it
I'd need a million tape measures

With a roof over my head
And with a warm duvet and bed
And my gleaming bike waiting in the shed

PlayStation, Game Boy, I've got the lot
I am so lucky to have what I've got

But there are some people who haven't got this
Their lives are so different
They have no bliss
No hidden treasures, no family to kiss.

Sam Plank (9)
St Thomas Garnet's School, Bournemouth

MY FIRST DAY

As I stood there standing
Outside my new school gate
I had this horrible feeling
That I was going to be late

The playground looked real empty
As I stood there at the gate
No more children standing
Oh no, I'm *really* late

And then I heard Mum shouting
It seemed so far away
I woke up with a startle
Today was the wrong day.

Joshua Bowmen (11)
St Thomas Garnet's School, Bournemouth

HIDDEN TREASURES

I am a little mermaid,
I live beneath the sea
And there are lots of
Hidden treasures that
Live beneath with me.

There are pearls
That shine a million dollars,
With bones and skulls
And sequin collars.

The seaweed sparkles
Like silver or rich gold,
Which I sometimes wish
That I could hold.

I have never seen
So many treasures
And it seems to me,
That they are rich pleasures.

Where will I find them?
Now I shall know,
To the bottom of the ocean
Is where I will go.

Natalie Rondeau (10)
St Thomas Garnet's School, Bournemouth

HIDDEN TREASURE

I have a hidden treasure
Not many people have
It's really not a secret
But a hidden treasure!

The hidden treasure is
The love that me and my family share
But the treasure above all
Is the gift of life itself!

Carina Hall-Nicolls (10)
St Thomas Garnet's School, Bournemouth

LEGOLAND

Legoland, Legoland, a great place to be
Until rain fell on me
Rain was a pain when we went on the train
Soaked and sodden, we marvelled at the sights

Dragon coaster, dragon coaster drove us insane
Going up and down, it dried us from the rain
Going up and down, round and round
Once you try it, you'll love it so much
You'll have to do it again and again

Football stadium, football stadium, so big and high
Watch the footballers kick the ball far
Going into the net and hear the crowd's roar
Some injuries here and there
Forget about them, enjoy the game

Lego train, Lego train, so exciting
Picking passengers up
And dropping them off
Steaming through the hills and looking at the views
Sounds so exciting, I'm almost there

Legoland, Legoland, I wish I could go there
It sounds so amusing, I have to go there.

Ross Browne (10)
St Thomas Garnet's School, Bournemouth

HIDDEN TREASURES

My hidden treasure is my family,
My sisters, my parents and my grandparents,
They're kind to me - and I love it!

My hidden treasure is my family,
I'm lucky I have my parents,
That they love both me and my sisters.

My grandparents are so nice to me - and I like it!
These are my hidden treasures,
My grandpa takes me on his motorcycle.

My treasure is my family
And God is a treasure too,
I am so rich in so many ways - are you?

Brookeleah Gossling (10)
St Thomas Garnet's School, Bournemouth

BEACHES

From blue to white,
The surf is alright,
Smashing on the rugged rocks.

A beach along the coast,
It's the one I love the most,
It's long and sandy.

I then found the Aussie crab,
It was not drab,
Its claws can pinch you.

Ryan Lewis (7)
St Thomas Garnet's School, Bournemouth

MUMMY AND DADDY

Mummy and Daddy are so nice,
They actually took me to the land of ice,
Where I met jolly old Santa, reindeer and sleigh,
I enjoyed every single day!

Mummy and Daddy are cool,
When we went on holiday I even missed some school,
Our holiday was in Spain, sunny, cool and bright
And with my brand new tan, I shone day and night.

Mummy and Daddy are so wild,
From country to country, from isle to isle.
Where places are sunny and places are grey,
I prefer it here in Bournemouth, so that is where I'll stay!

Rebecca Murphy (8)
St Thomas Garnet's School, Bournemouth

A CAT CAN...

A cat can creep,
A cat can sleep,
A cat can have olive-green eyes,
A cat can tell many lies,
A cat can be very small,
A cat can also fall,
A cat can play with wool,
A cat can be very cool,
A cat can have nine lives,
A cat can also smell chives,
A cat can relax at leisure,
But a cat cannot find . . .
Treasure!

Emily King (10)
St Thomas Garnet's School, Bournemouth

IMAGINE IF . . .

Imagine if there was only one season,
Would you like it to be -
The season when Jesus was betrayed for no reason
Or the season when Jesus was born?

Imagine if babies weren't born,
Would you and I exist?
Would there be any human race?

Imagine if Jesus wasn't born,
Would we all live in pain and hatred?

Imagine if Noah hadn't saved two
Of each kind of animal,
Would we have any companions?

Imagine if there was no time,
Would we forget to eat, sleep and go somewhere?

Imagine if all our crops died before we ate them,
What would we eat?

Imagine if our parents didn't work,
How would we pay for food?

Imagine if . . .

Catherine Hixson (10)
St Thomas Garnet's School, Bournemouth

THE STRUGGLE

I am struggling with this poem,
My mum keeps nagging
And the TV's going.
I can't hear myself thinking,
Sister's chewing,
People drinking.

Cars on the road,
Rain coming down.
Thinking of words,
Is making me frown.
I'd rather be in Lapland
Than doing this verse,
So if I do any more,
It will just get worse.

Bryony Cook (8)
St Thomas Garnet's School, Bournemouth

BURIED TREASURE

Jungly bushes,
Log pile snakes,
Crocodiles and alligators,
Swamps and lakes.

There's the X that marks the spot,
Hidden in a big brown box,
Jewels and treasures,
Sure brings great pleasures!

Trying to find it is the plot,
Clues and shapes
Show you the spot.

But please be careful,
Because all tricks
Are about,
If I were you,
I'd jolly well look out!

Maeve Orla Dunne (9)
St Thomas Garnet's School, Bournemouth

WHAT IS TREASURE?

What is treasure?
Where is it found?
Was it lost a long time ago?
Hidden in a chest,
With a lock and a key,
But what is inside?
I don't know,
So let's have a look
And then we will see!
Flashes of colour, shimmering bright
Light up the room.
Sparkling sapphires,
Glossy garnets,
Excellent emeralds,
Dazzling diamonds,
Precious pearls,
Hundreds of glittering gems,
Gold and silver coins,
All different sizes,
Beautiful tiaras and shining crowns,
Gorgeous jewellery of every type.
This is what we see
This is treasure!

Kristy O'Donnell (9)
St Thomas Garnet's School, Bournemouth

PLANETS

Planets are round,
Hot in places,
But cold in places.

Mars, Jupiter, Mercury,
Neptune and Venus,
And our planet
Earth.

Harry Leedham (10)
St Thomas Garnet's School, Bournemouth

MY LITTLE BROTHER

My little brother
Puts nappy cream on his face
And face cream on the wall!

My little brother
Wears socks on his hands
And Sellotapes gloves to his ears!

My little brother
Smears his beans on the cat
and eats Mum's flowers!

My little brother
Says 'boctor' for 'doctor'
And calls me 'bwother'!

My little brother
Steals Daddy's ties
And hangs them on the lamp!

My little brother -
There he goes with my homework diary!
Better stop him!
Bye!

Connor Groves-Waters (7)
St Thomas Garnet's School, Bournemouth

My Dog Digby

I've got a dog called Digby,
He smiles and barks at me,
Especially when I hide his toys,
He jumps around with glee.

I've got a dog called Digby,
He chews up all my shoes,
He snuffles about in my bedroom
And eats the Lego I lose.

I've got a dog called Digby,
He makes my mum quite mad,
She wags her finger and tells him off,
He looks so sorry and sad.

I've got a dog called Digby,
We go for nice long walks,
He trots along beside me,
I wish that he could talk.

I've got a dog called Digby,
He always likes a hug,
I let him sleep on the end of my bed,
Cos Digby's the dog I love.

Ben Waller (7)
St Thomas Garnet's School, Bournemouth

Ghosty, Ghosty

Ghosty, ghosty, where are you?
Spooking around with nothing to do.
Hiding in cupboards and floating up stairs,
Just waiting for someone to give them . . . *nightmares!*

Alex Thayne (7)
St Thomas Garnet's School, Bournemouth

WHERE IS THE TREASURE?

Where is the treasure?
Does anyone know?
I've been looking high and low,
But no one seems to know!

Where is the treasure?
Under the sand
Or could it be on another land?

Where is the treasure?
I think I know,
I think I saw it in a show.

There is the treasure!
That's where it was -
In the land of Oz!

Kapil Chauhan (8)
St Thomas Garnet's School, Bournemouth

BULLDOGS

Bulldogs are short and fat
They are mean and nasty
Now take that

We snarl and are vicious
But are not too mean
We can be very nice
But only in your dreams.

Julian Osei-Bonsu (7)
St Thomas Garnet's School, Bournemouth

I'VE GOT TWO CATS

Mogwai's a fluffball
And always lazy
Parky's black and white
And Parky's crazy

In the garden Parky sits on the fence
Mogwai sits on the wall
They dig out plants and roll around in the dirt
My dad doesn't like that!

Parky makes my mum happy
Parky makes my mum shout
Parky spins on the floor (he should be a stuntcat)
I like it when Parky sleeps on my bed

When things get to Mogwai they get a bit hard
She's spiky
She's soft
She's upstairs
She's downstairs
She's inside
She's out
She's a girl!

They're naughty
They're silly
They put their legs in the air
They fight
They scratch
And when they're asleep - knock, knock, who's there?

Paeris Giles (7)
St Thomas Garnet's School, Bournemouth

My Hidden Treasure

I came home from school
and rushed up the stairs
went in to my room
to check it was there

The most beautiful treasure
you ever did see
that Santa had bought
especially for me

It was hidden away
this treasure of mine
to keep from my sister
in case she should find

A bag of gold coins
so shiny and bright
delicious and tempting
oh, what a delight

But, oh to my horror
the coins were not there
I couldn't believe it
it just wasn't fair

In came my sister
oh, what a disgrace
just look at that chocolate
all over her face!

I now know what happened
to my treasure, so rare
my sister had eaten it
and *that's just not fair!*

Connor Rockey (9)
St Thomas Garnet's School, Bournemouth

TREASURE TRICKS

I've got a map for some treasure,
I followed it day and night,
To a cave at the end of the rainbow,
I was led.
There I met a bear,
He wasn't a very happy chappy,
He growled and went away,
I lit a fire and went to bed.
Morning light found me digging,
The treasure I must find.
Rocks and stones I moved,
At last - the treasure!
Gold and silver caught the light,
Rich! I was rich!
That smell - is it chocolate?
Oh no, my riches, my money!
Chocolates, just chocolates!

Tanja Wagner (9)
St Thomas Garnet's School, Bournemouth

SUMMER DREAM

Summer is hot and so warm
There is less chance for a storm
We play happily on the beach
Away from where the crashing waves reach
And when we see the sun's disappearing beam
We go home and that is the end of my dream.

David Passmore (7)
St Thomas Garnet's School, Bournemouth

ALIENS

Some people believe aliens are true,
Some people believe they are like me and you,
You never know, they could be watching you every night,
Just about the time the clock strikes midnight.
My brother believes they are five hundred feet tall,
With razor-sharp teeth that eat people whole.
Some aliens could come from Mars
And travel to all the stars,
But once when I was high up in a plane,
I looked outside and saw a yellow flame.
This I was sure was from a UFO,
But nobody will ever know.
So when you go to bed tonight,
Be sure to get tucked up tight
Or you could have a nasty fright.

William Porter (8)
St Thomas Garnet's School, Bournemouth

MY APPLE TREE

It lives in my garden
Its branches grow straight
The bark is bumpy
It grows at a very slow rate
Its apples are red
And a little bit green
We pick them all when they're ready to eat
They are delicious and a very nice treat.

Georgia Hill (8)
St Thomas Garnet's School, Bournemouth

SKYSCRAPER

I'm a skyscraper
Wow, look at me
I'm high and mighty
And what can you see?

Some people say I'm dumb
And I have stairs in my tum
Climb, climb, climb through my tum
Suddenly you're in my gum

I won't eat you
So don't be scared
I'm just full of offices
And people think of ideas there
And now, can you see, I'm not so dumb?

Iniubong Udoeyop (8)
St Thomas Garnet's School, Bournemouth

CATS

My cat is cute, small and quick,
She runs around our house.
She chases wool and balls and flies,
But never caught a mouse.
Her fur is long and fluffy brown,
It's almost like a rug
And when I hold her close to me,
She's really nice to hug.
Her eyes are bright and shiny,
She watches everything I do,
I love my cat, she is my friend,
I think she loves me too.

Mark Leedham (8)
St Thomas Garnet's School, Bournemouth

A Pirate Poem

Golden sands all around
Waves gently splashing
There came a great big pirate ship
With a captain giving out orders
He had a wooden leg which was shaped like a peg
They found a magic fish
Who gave them a wish
Their wish was treasure
But instead they were given a map
The map led them to a palm tree
Where they had to repeat me, me, me
And then a redd appeared
And said, 'Because you have been so conceited
You will have nothing at all!'
And a second later the redd disappeared and so did the treasure.

Jana Browne (9)
St Thomas Garnet's School, Bournemouth

The Messy Room

There was a girl called Jordan Norris
Who always made the same old promise
She said to her mum
'I will tidy my room from now on
I promise I will.'
But when her mum opened the door
She was angry at what she saw
Jordan had not kept her promise at all.

Jordan Norris (8)
St Thomas Garnet's School, Bournemouth

The Treasure In Tommy

His smile makes me fill with joy,
Because he is my little boy.
He says some very funny things
And laughs, giggles, cries and sings.
All Tommy does is play with his toys,
He likes girls but prefers the boys.
Sometimes he makes a great big din,
But in the end we always forgive him.

He's my treasure,
He's my joy,
He's my brother,
My little boy.

India Hall (8)
St Thomas Garnet's School, Bournemouth

Shipwrecked

It was a dark and stormy night
The wind was howling
It gave me such a fright
A great wave came towering over me and swept me off my feet
The icy water definitely needed some heat
Splashing and spluttering, I swam as hard as I could
What's that I hit? Hooray! It's a lump of wood
Clinging hold to my wooden float
It felt like it was my own special boat
Safely my special lump of wood carried me to shore
Now I was safe, I no longer needed my hidden treasure anymore.

Hannah Elcock (9)
St Thomas Garnet's School, Bournemouth

AS THE SEASONS GO BY

Spring, summer, autumn, winter,
The seasons go by,
Spring, summer, autumn, winter,
Another year flies.

Spring has blossom and flowers,
They've coped,
Summer has hot days,
I hope.

Autumn has lost leaves,
Where's my rake?
Winter has snow,
That's just fake.

The seasons come,
Have some fun,
The seasons go,
It's sad to know,
But they will come again.

Rachel Dingley (10)
St Thomas Garnet's School, Bournemouth

TREASURE

T reasures gold,
R ough and old.
E verlasting,
A fter time passing.
S hiny and shimmering,
U ltra glimmering.
R eady to spend,
E xtra special gleaming gold!

Hannah Pickup (9)
St Thomas Garnet's School, Bournemouth

THE TREASURE IN THE SEA

Down in the ocean hidden below
Lies a vessel full of treasure all on its own
Not stirring or moving or making a sound
Only the fish, the shark and the octopus
Are swimming around

They are the ones which I know
The secrets hidden within this tale
They witnessed an event which was so queer
Something came from the sky
And sunk so near

Was it a galleon or ship which they say
Or could it be the Titanic
Lying on the dark ocean floor?

George Soan (10)
St Thomas Garnet's School, Bournemouth

MY FAMILY

My name is Nathan, football is my game,
If I lose, it's a really big shame.
My brother's called Luke, he's a really cool dude,
At least he is when he's not in a mood.
My sister is Hannah, she's very arty
And in the evenings, she loves to party.
Sue's my mum, she loves to sing
Andy's my dad, the trumpet's his thing.
That's my family, they're a really great bunch,
Especially when they take me out to lunch.

Nathan Watkins (8)
The Epiphany School

THE SNOWFLAKE DOLPHIN

The snowflake dolphin was a wonderful creature,
It was all different colours and had an obscene feature.
Its obscene feature was shimmery blue,
It swims in the sea without a clue,
If you're ever to see this thing
Always be sure to listen to it sing.
Its amazing voice has a sound of its own,
When you come across it, this will be shown.
For this mystical animal has a challenge for you,
You will only succeed if you know what to do,
This challenge consists of a magical power,
You might gain it in the bath or even in the shower.
When this power comes to your body,
You will know what to do,
Now it lies in your destiny, to do whatever comes to you.

Natasha Daysh (9)
The Epiphany School

SHARK ATTACK!

A shark came out the water
Said he'd eat me whole.
He really should have caught me,
Instead he ate the pole.
But just a minute later,
The shark came back for more,
But this time he caught me,
He even ate the core.

Aaron Trowbridge (9)
The Epiphany School

MY MAGIC FRIEND

I've got a magic friend,
He is really cool.
I take him everywhere,
He even comes to school.

He can do really naughty things,
Like lift up skirts and pull hair.
He even lifted up the teacher's skirt
And he gave her quite a scare!

But now he is a good cat
And stays home with Mum.
He eats and sleeps all day
And then we have lots of fun.

I've got a magic friend,
He is really cool.
I take him everywhere,
But I don't take him to school.

Mandy Cronk (9)
The Epiphany School

THE GOOD THINGS OF WINTER

Robin in the tree branch,
Stoat in the snow,
Snowflakes flying through the sky,
Cos wintertime is here.

Fires going crackle, crackle,
Playing in the snow,
Icicles hanging from the houses,
Cos wintertime is here.

Red berries, green holly,
Frost all around,
Terrific sights,
Starry nights,
Cos wintertime is here.

So enjoy your winter,
While it still is here,
Because it does not last
All the way through the year!

Simone Claire Vibert (9)
The Epiphany School

SOUNDS ALL AROUND

In the sitting room I can hear . . .

The crying of the baby
The chatting on the telephone
The music on the stereo
The purring of the cat

In the kitchen I can hear . . .

The bubbling of the boiler
The humming of the fridge
The scraping of the knife
The clatter of the plates

In the main hall I can hear . . .

The notes of the piano
The creaking of the doors
The shutting of the door
Everything!

Zack Reed (9)
The Epiphany School

MY BED

My bed is big
My bed is tall
My bed has lots of things
But that's not all

My bed is cosy
My bed is nice
I love my bed
So take my advice

My bed just sits there
Doing what it does
Off goes the alarm clock
Buzz
Buzz
Buzz

The new day starts
It's quarter to ten
Then in the morning
The buzz goes off again
Buzz.

Alex Lee (8)
The Epiphany School

THE ANIMALS

The pecking of a peacock,
The larking of a llama,
The slithering of a snake,
The flapping of a flamingo.

The hooting of a hawk,
The gulping of a goldfish,
The teasing of a Tasmanian devil,
The crawling of a crab.

The tottering of a turtle,
The gulping of a goldfish,
The reaction of a robin,
The laughing of a lapwing.

The animals are here,
The animals are dear,
The animals are here, my dear.

Benjamin Clayton (9)
The Epiphany School

CORN LIKES THE SUN

The farmer works hard
Night and day
After that
What does he say?

Corn likes the sun
Corn likes the rain
Then once more it's chopped again

The farmer works hard
Day and night
He works in the evening
And the morning light

Corn likes the sun
Corn likes the rain
Then once more it's chopped again

The farmer goes to bed
And in his sleep
Dreams about
Counting his sheep.

Sasha Jones (9)
The Epiphany School

MUM'S SOLD ME TO A SHOP

Mum's sold me to a shop,
She says I'm absolutely useless!
I'm being sold for just £10,
The sign says:
For sale,
10 years old,
Never been used,
Been a mascot for England,
Always smiling,
Very good at football,
You will need a washing machine for weeks of
Washing his football kit.
The guarantee is: If he needs a new football kit,
We will buy it for him,
Term and conditions: Guarantee only lasts 12 months
Any takers?
I said any takers?
Please, please, please,
Take this boy off my hands,
He's reduced, now only £5.

Emily Apps (9)
The Epiphany School

THE RIBBON

I know a lady who's got a ribbon,
She got it and she looked at it.
It reminded her of her daughter,
Who died in the war.

She got it in her daughter's hair box,
It was the first ribbon she ever had.
She looked at it,
She kept it in her drawer.

Her daughter wore it on her fifth birthday party,
The ribbon was pink and purple
And it matched her daughter's party dress.

Edita Parkinson (8)
The Epiphany School

HARVEST POEM

Corn likes the sun, corn likes the rain,
Then once more it's chopped again.

The farmer works hard
In the sunny light,
He harvests all day
And harvests all night.

Corn likes the sun, corn likes the rain,
Then once more it's chopped again.

The farmer works hard,
Night and day,
After that,
What do we say?

Corn likes the sun, corn likes the rain,
Then once more it's chopped again.

The farmer works hard,
Day and night,
He works in the evening
And the morning light.

Corn likes the sun, corn likes the rain,
Then once more it's chopped again.

Hannah Featherstone (9)
The Epiphany School

CAR SOUNDS

The slamming of the door
The turning of the key
The beeping of the horn
The starting of the engine

The ticking of the indicator
The whirring of the window
The screeching of the wheel
The swishing of the windscreen wipers

The slamming of the boot
The talking of the children
The clicking of the seatbelt
The halting of the brake.

Grant Wells (10)
The Epiphany School

THE SPOOKY HOUSE

There once was a spooky house near the prom
That everybody ran away from,
Once they looked at it, their eyes were beaming,
They always ran away screaming.
The ghosts come out at night,
They give a really big fright!
The bats take a gigantic bite,
The people say, 'What an awful sight.'
When it's morning, everybody's yawning
And that's a warning for every monster
To go back to sleep!

William Handford (9)
The Epiphany School

HIDDEN TREASURES

Right at the back I saw it,
Deep in the dark of the closet,
In the box I found my treasure,
Where it gives me hours of pleasure,
Action Man toys,
Which I share with the boys
And a Spirograph to draw swirls,
This I leave for the girls,
There are noisy guns and bouncy balls,
These are the ones that drive my mummy up the walls,
I even found a cricket bat,
This is just for me and my stepdad,
One day I will stop the Action Man battle
And swap it all for some grown-up fishing tackle,
But for now I will put away my treasure
And hope someday it will give my children pleasure.

Samuel Walkling-Talbot (9)
The Epiphany School

THE BIRTHDAY CARD

I know a lady
Who's got a birthday card
She found it on the floor
Outside somebody's house
It was somebody who died
During the war
A bomb exploded
The house was destroyed
And now the lady
Keeps the card and remembers.

Chloe Runnacles (8)
The Epiphany School

SOUNDS

There are millions and millions of sounds in our world
What would we be without them?

No squealing from a squeaking mouse,
No roaring from the lions,
No laughter from within our house,
All is silent and still.

The wind doesn't rustle amongst the trees,
The hailstones fall silently,
No whoosh of rockets on Bonfire Night,
No noise heard as the waves crash in the sea.

Oh sounds come back,
Oh sounds, oh please,
Our world is not the same without you.

Natalie Dyke (9)
The Epiphany School

I KNOW A BOY CALLED HARRY

I know a boy called Harry,
Who is rather mad,
I know a boy called Harry,
Who is very bad.
I know a boy called Harry,
Who makes people sad,
I know a boy called Harry,
Who is a jolly lad.

Jade Evans (8)
The Epiphany School

When I Was Christened

When I was Christened
They held me up
And poured some water
Out of a cup

The trouble was
It fell on me
And I and water
Don't agree

A lot of Christeners
Stood and listened
To let the know
That I was Christened!

Natalie George (9)
The Epiphany School

Ancient Egypt

Egypt has a lot of sand
Camels travel over land
Hieroglyphics on the walls
Everyone at the Pharaoh's call
Slaves that built the pyramids high
Sphinx looks up towards the sky
People in the River Nile
Tutankhamun ruled a while
Mummies asleep inside their tomb
Do not awaken them from their doom.

Catherine Lee-Smith (9)
The Epiphany School

IN THE DEPTHS OF LOST PROPERTY

One day I went to the servery
To have a quick look in Lost Property,
My mother sent me, as mothers do,
To find my lost glove, but I'll give you a clue

What I found in the box
Was nothing of mine,
But these are the things
That I happened to find . . .

One boy's pair of trainers,
A girl's pair of shorts,
An old, scuffed-up football
That boys used for sports,
A faded, ripped baseball cap
That had seen better days,
A fluffy toy horse which
You press and it neighs,
Four smelly old socks
Not one of a pair,
A once-pretty doll
That had lost all her hair,
A chewing gum wrapper,
Nine dirty school ties,
An old purple lunch box
Labelled Keith Wise.

I haven't found anything of mine, nothing at all,
If you find a grey glove, then please give me a call.

Hannah Dibden (9)
The Epiphany School

THE MAGICAL DOOR

There it was, there it stood,
I was shaking, I put down my hood,
I reached for the handle and guess what I saw?
A growling lion sniffing the air
And oh, my sister combing her hair.
I saw tall, tall towers,
Colourful flowers,
Rainbow stripes,
Smoky pipes.
My sister said, 'I hope you like it.'
I said, 'It is quite a delight.'
So anyway, I searched the place,
I met the lion face to face,
He let out a roar,
I grabbed the door.
But then I realised, this place is only pretend,
I could walk round for hours, it would never end.
I said to my sister,
'This place is so fun!'
'Trust me, my brother, it's just begun.'
So I walked around with no cares,
Then stood before me, some wild, fast hares.
There was a meal set out on the table,
Instead of Sky television, there was cable.
I thought I was in the door,
But instead, I woke up Monday morning,
I was in my bed.

Mary Johnstone (9)
The Epiphany School

THE GHOST TRAIN

In the ghost train, round the track,
Going along, then doubling back.
In the ghost train, in the dark,
Scary faces, what a lark!

Creepy noises, sounds of fright,
In the ghost train, in the night.
But what's this? Our speed decreases,
The ghost train slows, then movement ceases!

Sitting alone, it feels so scary,
What I need is a good fairy.
Lord, I promise to say my prayers,
Take me home, I hate these fairs!

Help - a ghost, I heard a sound!
Lord, I pray that I'll be found.
Take me home, I will be good,
I'll say my prayers like angels should!

Wait a minute . . . the train is starting,
Lord, it looks like we're departing!
Yes, I'm going home to bed,
Please ignore what I just said!

Claudia Poole (10)
The Epiphany School

ELIZABETH I

Elizabeth I was a queen
She was terribly, terribly mean
She cut off their heads
And chopped them to shreds
And then they were never again seen.

Elizabeth Kimber (9)
The Epiphany School

UNDER THE SEA

Under the sea,
There are unexpected creatures lurking about
Where nobody has ever been before
Under the sea
Schools of tiny fish swim around the seabed
Looking for some dinner
Under the sea
There are beautiful dolphins that glide across the water
Under the sea
Elegant sea horses explore their world
While the jellyfish also search for food

Under the sea
The fish race
With the mermaid's magic
It's a wonderful place!

Jessica Saracino (9)
The Epiphany School

I'M STUCK!

Scratch, scratch, I'm scratching my head,
Scratch, scratch, soon it's going to be raw and red.
Scribble, scribble, everyone else finds it so easy,
Easy peasy, lemon squeasy!
Click, click, I can almost hear them thinking,
Scratch, scratch, click, click, scratch, scratch,
Click, click, click, click, clunk, I've had an idea,
Ding-a-ling-ling, oh no the bell for play, the lesson has ended.

Genevieve Martin (9)
The Epiphany School

THE MUDDY MATCH

The rain is falling very hard
And both teams have to be on their guard
England are playing in shirt of white
And Brazil's yellow shirts are really bright
It's almost half-time, the score is 2-1
Owen has scored and is having some fun
Brazil attack and finally score
And at half-time it's a 2-2 draw
The match goes on and on and on
Where has Beckham gone?
Screech! Goes the whistle for a free kick
The Brazil players are feeling sick
Beckham scores to put England 3-2 up
So England win the World Cup!

Aron Shute (9)
The Epiphany School

HORSEY LOVE

Green Cottage is where I like to go, to see the ponies that I know,
I muck out the stable, lead and sweep and I work hard every week,
In the rain, heat or snow, I don't care, I will still go.

I love riding and jumping with my friends and wish the lesson
                                                will never end,
Neris is my favourite pony, I would love her to be mine, if only!

I love the ponies, each and every one,
Some of them are cheeky and some of them are fun,
I take them to the field, they gallop off and play, until I see
                                        them another day.
Goodbye horses for another week.

Natasha Triggs (9)
The Epiphany School

Dinosaurs In My Garden

I was digging in my garden and I struck something hard,
It was dirty, white and large.
I had to use my daddy's spade to get it out,
It was long and very heavy.

I cleaned it in some soapy water and made it shine like new,
It looked like a bone.
I looked it up in my book at home,
It was a dinosaur bone.

I took it to the dinosaur museum, who said it was a treasure,
It was from a Tyrannosaurus rex.
I asked if I could keep it,
It was a hidden treasure, but they said yes.

Jason Everitt (8)
The Epiphany School

The Helmet

I know a woman who's got a helmet
She got it from her dad
And every day she looks at it
And knows that he is glad

That same old woman still keeps that hat from 1945
And even now she still wishes he was still alive
Now she puts it in her drawer, all made of pine
And that reminds her of 1939

That old war was very sad
A lot of children lost their dad
But lucky her, she has a reminder of her dad
It puts a tear in her eye, so very sad . . .

Sian Burton (9)
The Epiphany School

Your Ideas About Love...

What do you think about love?
(Pass the bucket please!)
Some say it's a peaceful dove,
Others, a load of mushy peas!

What do you think about love?
A big kiss and a huge hug?
But maybe others think a glove
Is more interesting than the love bug.

But, we all fall in love at some time,
So don't start hating it now.
It's not as sour as lemons and limes,
But as sweet as a daisy, there now!

Charlotte Harwood (11)
The Epiphany School

A Ribbon

I know a lady who's got a ribbon
She's had it since she was young
It was the first ribbon she ever had
She got it from her dad
Before he went to war
But now he is dead

I know a lady who's got a ribbon
She put it on a grave
Her dad's grave
She goes there every Sunday
She looks at her ribbon
To remember him from the past.

Ella Owen (8)
The Epiphany School

THE THING

Down deep in the depths of the sea
A monster came and it ate me
As it went and ate my feet
I heard *'Gurgle, gurgle, human meat!'*

Then it goes and bites off my head
I'm lying down on the seabed
And it goes and eats my leg
'No! No more! *Please!'* I beg

There I am, in its tum
I can hear it saying, 'Yum!'
He is talking to another thing
Thing just ate my brother, Ling.

Zoe Escott (10)
The Epiphany School

MY OWN HOME

What we have for tea, I'll never know,
Just then *ping!* Goes the microwave, our dinner's on the go.

'Miaow,' goes the cat, she's waiting for her dinner,
Nan says, 'Shush, you're not getting thinner.'

The washing machine goes zoom, zoom, zoom,
While the doorbell and door knocker go rat-a-tat-tat and
                                                      ring-a-ting-ting.

The fridge goes hum, hum, hum and the taps still run, run, run.

The stairs are so wooden and light brown,
That they're not very fun to go bumpety-bump down.

Francesca Simpson-Rathbone (9)
The Epiphany School

MY GRANDAD

My grandad's very funny
Especially when we're out spending money
He's always very brainy
Even when it's very rainy

That's my grandad

My grandad goes to work with the trains
And never shows any sign of strains
I never turn down a trip to see him
And he never turns down a hair trim

That's my grandad

My grandad's got a very nice house
And it doesn't store a single mouse
Even though he's got problems with his chest
I'd never turn him down, as he is the best.

That's my grandad.

Samantha Fear (10)
The Epiphany School

THE HERO

I know a man who got a medal,
He found it on his friend,
He keeps it for remembrance,
For now his friend is dead.

He cried when he saw it,
He couldn't stop.
It brings back lots of happy memories
Of his childhood.

The two grew up together at school,
They were in the same class.
They always played together,
They were the best of friends.

The medal was very special to him,
He kept it very close,
He thought his friend was a hero
Because he died for his country.

Lawrence Warner Green (8)
The Epiphany School

IN THE KITCHEN

Ping! Goes the microwave
Our dinner's ready to eat
Swoosh said the washing machine
Joining in with the beat

Scrape! Goes the kitchen knife
Spreading jam with a slush
This jam on toast looks perfectly lush

Ring! Goes the timing clock
The rice crispy cakes are set
And I've been screeching
'Mum, are these cakes ready yet?'

Whoosh! Goes the kettle
Making the cat jump
The cat flew over the kitchen sink
And landed with a thump.

Gemma Sandell (9)
The Epiphany School

UNDER THE SEA

Down deep under the sea
A whale came when I was watching TV
It swallowed me whole
Like a fish in a bowl

I was in his tum
And I saw his mum
He had eaten his mummy
He said she was yummy

Then he spat me out
Through his water spout
It was his wish
That I had tasted like a fish.

Leanna Bartlett (10)
The Epiphany School

THE RIBBON

I used to know a lady
Who had a ribbon,
She got it from her dad
Before he went to war.
Every day she wears it,
In memory of him.
She used to keep it under her bed,
She got it when she was two years old.
She still wears it now,
Although she is in Heaven
And in her hair it is.

Charlotte Cleere (8)
The Epiphany School

THE STARS

The stars are so bright,
They sparkle at night,
Winking in-between,
They say 'Hello,'
And give us a glow,
It's a starry dream.

Kate Sidwick (9)
The Epiphany School

TEDDY BEAR

A little girl
Got a teddy bear
From her dad,
He went to war
And did not return,
She always cuddles it.

Lauren Gatcum (8)
The Epiphany School

CATS

I would love a cat,
Why do I say that?
I think cats are lovely,
When I see one I feel all bubbly.

Stephanie Duggan (9)
The Epiphany School

LITTLE HARRY

Harry is my hamster,
My favourite little pet.

I love my little Harry,
Ever since we met!

I love my little Harry,
He's small and sweet and round.

When I cuddle little Harry,
He makes a little sound.

I love my little Harry,
His whiskers are so cute.

My favourite thing about Harry,
He sleeps in my left boot.

Oh, I love my little Harry,
My bestest little friend.

But when he's running on that wheel,
He drives me round the bend!

Alexandra Lauren Ridout (9)
The Epiphany School

BOMB SHRAPNEL

I know a man who has got a bit of bomb shrapnel
He found it in the war
This bit of shrapnel knocked a brick out by his front door
He keeps it so he can remember his friends who died in the war.

Shaun Burbidge (9)
The Epiphany School

SWEEP!

My dog Sweep
Is a poodle
She can run while
Eating noodles

She is black
And she's cool
That's a fact
But she does drool

She always goes mad
After her bath
She chases my dad
And makes us all laugh

She's got energy all day
She never stops to catch her breath
She'll never be a stray
She'll never be a chef (that's for sure)

My dog Sweep
Is the best
She's a loveable poodle
But she's better than the rest.

Katy Brothers (11)
The Epiphany School

MONSTERS

Monsters big, monsters small
Monsters fat, monsters tall
Monsters wide, monsters strong
Monsters really getting on your gong.

Jake Ashley Carton (8)
The Epiphany School

THE TEDDY

I know a girl who's got a teddy,
She's kept it from the war.
She looks at it every now and then,
Remembering the war.
She loves it more than anything,
Because she remembers her mum and dad
From the war.

Sophia Moorehouse (8)
The Epiphany School

THE PHOTO

I know a man who's got a photo
He found it in the loft
He keeps it under his pillow
Since his brother died
Every year he gets it out on the pier
To remember him.

Adam Dean (8)
The Epiphany School

THE KEY

I know a man who's got a key,
It was his house key, when it was war time.
It is a bit bent and rusty now,
But it still reminds him of the war.
The house got bombed, tragically.

Zachary Bradley (9)
The Epiphany School

The Flower

I know a woman who's got a flower,
She got it from her dad,
She put it in the middle of a Bible,
It reminds her of the man,
It reminds her of his love and care,
It reminds her of his smell,
She looks at it every day,
She will never forget him.

Naomi Davies (9)
The Epiphany School

The Doll

I know a lady who's got a doll,
She found it in Green Lane,
She took it home to remind her
Of her mum and dad in the war,
She played with it
And she put it near a tree,
She sees it every year.

Zara Baxter (8)
The Epiphany School

The Water Flask

I know a man who's got a water flask
He found it in a mess
Nobody knows whose it was
It brings him sad memories of the war
Of all the friends he lost.

Zak Sutcliffe (8)
The Epiphany School

THE MEDAL

I know a man who's got a medal,
He found it in a field,
His friend gave it to him before he died.
He cried and cried,
He couldn't stop crying,
Then he was dying, until he was dead.
His friend took the medal,
To remember both his friends.

Lewis Paul Vincent (8)
The Epiphany School

GUESS WHO?

This is what my mum sounds like
When she tells me off for not doing things,
Here she goes again,
Guess who doesn't tidy their room?
Guess who doesn't do the washing-up?
Guess who doesn't help do dinner?
Guess who doesn't do their homework?
You!

Zoë Emma Beale (10)
The Epiphany School

THE RIBBON

I know a man who's got a ribbon
He found it on the road
He hung it upon the wall
It belonged to a girl
He used to know.

Adam Proudley (9)
The Epiphany School

HIDDEN TREASURE

In the attic from the drawer,
I heard a loud, scary roar,
I thought I was dreaming,
Then I saw something shining, beaming.
Was it a ghost? A TV host?
A glow-worm? My sister squirm?
I heard a loud, scary roar,
In the attic from the drawer.

I opened the drawer as slow as I could,
As slow as I dare, as slow as I would,
I looked inside and it looked creepy,
Gave me a funny feeling - made me sleepy.
I shook away the sleepy feeling,
Inside the drawer the sides were peeling,
Inside I saw a real old book,
I only had a little look.
I slammed it shut as quick as I could,
As quick as I dare, as quick as I would.

Mum said that it had been well-hidden,
When Grandad died we were forbidden
To look, to peep, to see inside,
But now with my mum by my side,
Within the book was hidden treasure,
It was to give us years of pleasure.
To remember Grandad how he was,
I asked Mum why, she said, 'Because.'
It never was my sister squirm or a glow-worm,
It never was a ghost or even a TV host,
I never did find out what made that roar,
In the attic from that drawer.

Michael Homer (11)
Upton Junior School

HIDDEN TREASURE

Hidden under your feet right now
Hidden under the ground right now
Down, down, beneath the ground
Something old
Something new

Hidden under your bed right now
Hidden under the car right now
Down, down, beneath the ground
Something shines
Something valuable

Hidden under the sea right now
Hidden under the reef right now
Something shines in the sand
Something shines in the sea

Down, down, under the sea
Down, down, beneath the fish
Something in the sea, I'm sure of it
Treasures, I'm sure of it

Hidden under the sky
Hidden in the clouds
Hidden under the stars
Hidden under the moon

Down, down, under the bed
Down, down, under the floor.

Stephanie Stokes (11)
Upton Junior School

Hidden Treasures

The treasures are out there, somewhere in the world,
Unknown to existence, unable to be heard.

High or low, the treasures may lay,
We search and search every day.

No such luck have we had,
They may be found by good or bad.

I may find it, I may not,
It may be in my sister's cot.

It lies beneath the ocean deep,
It may be treasure you don't want to keep.

It may be in my hamster's cage,
It may lay hidden on a book page.

It might be silver, it might be gold,
It might be new, it might be old.

It may be floating around in some soup,
It may be in a chicken coup.

Finally . . .

Wow! I've found the treasure,
Oh, what a pleasure.

Now I can have a big rest,
Knowing I beat the rest.

Zoë Swinburn (10)
Upton Junior School

HIDDEN TREASURE

In the darkness, I lay awake,
My stomach says it wants more cake.
As I make my way downstairs,
I see a twinkle in sight
That shines so very bright.
What can it be? I said to myself,
Going down on my knees.
I picked up the glistening thing,
In an instant, I knew it was a ring.
The ruby was as red as a rose,
The rim as smooth as glass,
As I put the ring back with no sound,
I knew it was treasure I'd found.
Tiptoeing my way to the fridge,
I took a chunk of my favourite cake
And made my way back to bed,
I know I'd find my best ted.

Sandeep Marwaha (11)
Upton Junior School

HIDDEN TREASURES

What is a hidden treasure?
Is it pirates' treasure?
Is it the land of Eldorado?
Is it a lost city of love?
What is a hidden treasure?

What is a hidden treasure?
Is it a letter from a lost loved one?
Is it a chest of silver?
Is it the love digging into two people?
What is a hidden treasure?

What is a hidden treasure?
Is it the love of a man and a woman?
Is it the love of a newborn baby?
Is it the love of your girlfriend?
What is a hidden treasure?

What is a hidden treasure?
Is it the sight of watching the sunset?
Is it the sight of watching dawn break?
Is it the sight of counting stars
What is a hidden treasure?

Ashleigh Pegg (11)
Upton Junior School

BOTTOM OF THE SEA

H   iding deep, deep down
I   n the bottom of the sea
D   ucking in and out
D   ipping and diving
E   very size and colour
N   ever seen but sometimes heard

T   ropical with flashy colours
R   ushing away from their enemy
E   very shade
A   mazing and shimmering
S   ailors hear their mournful cry
U   nder the waves so high
R   eturn to their safe homes
E   ating mackerel for their supper
S   eals and their treasure.

Kym Gibbs (10)
Upton Junior School

TREASURE IS EVERYWHERE

H idden treasure? Is there really such a thing?
I s there really a treasure inside you?
D o we really know what treasure is?
D o we treasure life's possessions more than life itself?
E arth's treasures, is it natural or manmade?
N ew life or old wisdom, which is the ultimate treasure?

T rees give us oxygen but do we appreciate its value?
R ivers run rapidly what can we give back?
E ver increasing wars, is power a real treasure?
A frowning expression, could it be changed?
S miles, can they touch the world?
U nder the sea, do treasures still lie?
R ubies and riches, what are they worth?
E verybody stand, stare, be thankful and appreciate.

Daniel Rose (10)
Upton Junior School

SPARK IN THE DARK

They
say the
world's best
treasures are the
pyramids of Egypt.
But why has a crumbling
mound of cursed rock captured
the Earth's mind? Why aren't new-
born babies the little rubies of the world?
Why aren't the dusty films that reveal the secrets
of early childhood the magic of our lives? *Why aren't
each and every one of us a spark in the dark for the planet?*

Jenny Wigmore (10)
Upton Junior School

ANYONE'S DREAM

As I jump with joy in the waves,
Suddenly I see some mysterious caves.
I gently glide across the deep blue sea,
But when I spot a shark, I quickly flee.
I'm so frightened - very tense,
This is what made me suddenly sense,
A fish swims across my body - so sleek,
I get distracted - an awful reek.
It's coming from the caves - I know it is,
There's something shiny, oh what a bliss!
I make my way back to the site,
A mistake was made, I tried to bite.
There's piles and piles of shiny things,
They are so hard - there's even some rings!
I quickly glide round the bends,
I have to tell the news to my friends!

Faye Mitchell (11)
Upton Junior School

TREASURE

I wonder what treasure really is?
  I wonder what it's like to hold it?
    I wonder if you can hold it or is it someone?
      I wonder if we all have treasure?
        I wonder what my treasure is?
          I wonder if it's my home, food or my family?
        I wonder, I wonder what treasure really is?

Ellen House (11)
Upton Junior School

UNKNOWN TREASURES

U nder the sea are treasures unknown,
N ow are those still hidden,
K ings in countries wonder,
N ature has stories, upon words of truth,
O f course people still search,
W ondering about the treasures
N ow hidden beyond imagination!

T elling stories about them,
R eassure people in imagination,
E very day people grow eager,
A mid curiosities
S earching are they still?
U nder seas and on land
R eassuring themselves of what is hiding,
E ach day is a wait, but
S earching, still searching for what is hidden!

Shontelle Young (11)
Upton Junior School

SOMETHING HIDDEN

Hidden under your feet right now,
Hidden under the ground right now,
Something under there, under the ground,
Something valuable, something round.

Hidden under your bed right now,
Hidden under your house right now,
Something beneath the floor,
Something beneath the door.

Hidden inside your mind right now,
Hidden in the sea right now,
Something in the sky,
Something drifting by.

Hidden around us right now,
Hidden inside us right now,
Something that's not silver or gold,
Something that's not cold.

Hidden, but bountiful - love.

Harriet Davis (10)
Upton Junior School

Hidden Treasures

H idden somewhere is my dog, my friend
I s my dog in the sea or did it go looking for me?
D id my dog run away?
D id my dog find another home?
E veryone I know around me has a dog, I'm so sad!
N othing can replace her.

T here's nothing like my dog to make me warm inside.
R eading books about dogs makes me happy!
E very time I'm down, I play with my dog, she cheers me up.
A dog is for life and not just for birthdays or Christmas!
S ascha, my dog, is clever and smart!
U nderstanding and trust are what we have for each other.
R unning and jumping are things she likes to do!
E veryone loves her,
'S pecially me!

Nikki Turner (10)
Upton Junior School

CAUTIOUSLY CREEPING

Cautiously creeping through the gloomy cave,
We come across a crumbling body,
Then a groan comes from behind us,
As we come across a bone-made door.

Silently crawling through the slimy mud,
We see a piece of shining rock,
Then we hear the frightening boom of the gong,
As we dodge the soldiers, one by one.

Fearfully darting along the winding road,
Jumping over boiling pools of lava,
Closing in on our destination,
The *Tomb of Doom!*

Hannah Powis (11)
Upton Junior School

HIDDEN TREASURE

L ost in a wilderness of books and toys,
O ver the mountain of clothes,
S urviving on leftovers,
T ravelling by night.

H anging by his claws on the curtains,
A rranging a nest for the day.
M ishaps await around every corner.
S ilently sleeping by day.
T unnelling through his master's bedclothes,
E ntering a maze of tubes,
R eunited with his master at last.

Matt Mosley (11)
Upton Junior School

UNDER MY FLOORBOARDS

Under my floorboards,
A mouse scampers,
A piece of dust flies.
Under my floorboards,
Something catches my eye,
Something shiny.
Under my floorboards,
There is a box,
It is metal.
Under my floorboards,
In the box, some jewels,
In the box, precious pictures of my family,
That's what's under my floorboards.

Matthew Knight (11)
Upton Junior School

LOST HAMSTER

L   ost somewhere on a grassy plain,
O   verhead it looks like rain.
S   illy boy brought me out here to play,
T   hen the ice cream man came and he ran away.

H   e'll come back, of that I'm sure,
A   fter all, he's left me here before.
M   um told him not to take me out,
S   omeone's cat might be out and about.
T   here he is now with his lolly in his hand,
E   verybody's happy except me in the sand.
R   ight, I'm going kids - I'll never understand!

Chris Emerson (10)
Upton Junior School

MY TREASURES WAITING

Life has been hard for a long time now,
The cruel frost of the morning
Bites my tail
And forbids me my wanted sleep.

Hunting my treasures,
I can no longer remember the warmth
And satisfaction of that lovely treasure.

The restless spirit inside me needs consoling,
So come back,
My glowing treasure.

The treasure has come;
Spring, where the sun smiles upon me
And the Earth is just waking.

I was right, I told myself,
I had survived the long wait,
New life, new treasure.

I flicked open one eye,
Strange, but the crisp night air seemed different,
There was a whisper in the wind.

My treasure, spring, had arrived.

Kathryn Cullen (10)
Upton Junior School

LIFE

Gone are the days of yesteryear,
When we were young and without a care.
A time gone by, so long ago,
All that's left is a memory and a tear.

Today we work for tomorrow's dream,
We sit and learn all manner of things.
Our sums, our words and our growing up,
For when tomorrow comes, we want the dream.

Kristopher Jones (10)
Upton Junior School

HIDDEN TREASURE

A ll gold you want
B rilliant shiny gold and silver
C ars made out of gold
D ulcet magic clock to go anywhere you want
E verywhere you want, when you want
F ar away from home as you want to be
G old is cool and shiny
H urricanes will stop with a shiny, magic clock
I n the future everything will be made out of gold
J ourneys will last two seconds with a magic ball
K illing treasure is in a separate box, never to be opened
L arge poisonous adders will never kill you
M ammoths won't kill
N asty people will be poor
O lympic stadium will be made out of gold
P oor people will be rich
Q uick and quiet with a magic marble
R ich and wealthy will be like normal people
S tealing will not be known because everyone will be rich
T alented people will be rich
U V W X Y and Z is for my secret treasure that will unfold when all my secrets have been told.

Danny Hudson (11)
Upton Junior School

WHERE?

     H idden treasures are out there, somewhere out there in the world.
     I n a cupboard or under a tree, but where?
     D own, down, down in the ground,
     D own . . . down . . . down . . . waiting to be found.
     E ven I cannot tell you where.
     N o one has discovered it's there.

     T reasures are out there, but where in the world?
a   R e they close to you or are they faraway
or E ven on the moon?
     A magical thing hidden somewhere
     S its waiting to be found
yo U could discover it, possibly not,
     R esting in a corner hidden from you
     E xciting to find it hidden away
it' S magic waiting to be discovered!

Rebecca Pierce (10)
Upton Junior School

HIDDEN TREASURES

Hidden treasure is a shooting star,
Hidden treasure is a crown from afar,
Hidden treasure is a piece of gold,
Hidden treasure is a fold,
Hidden treasure is some sea,
Hidden treasure is a flea.

Hidden treasure is a very good thing,
Hidden treasure gives a ping,
Hidden treasure is wonderful,
Hidden treasure is beautiful,
Hidden treasure, hidden treasure,
The most important hidden treasure is . . .
Love!

Sam Sweeney (10)
Upton Junior School

In The Tree House

H idden in the tree house, up in the tree
I s it me or can I see?
D inted in the moonlit wall
D oes it really call
E nchanted watch - enchanted treasure
N othing could give me more pleasure

T o the top of the ladder I climb
R unning, running to see what I can find
E ntering the tree house, I jump up off the ground
A h! It's a rumbling sound
S haking like the trembling tree
U nder the moonlit wall, an enchanted watch I see
R eaching out cautiously - I gasp
E ven the ticking sounds were crystal-clear
S eriously though - you would not believe me -
　my enchanted treasure is right near me.

Robert Hatchard (10)
Upton Junior School

HIDDEN TREASURES

H idden under my floorboards was something
I n my floorboards was something suspicious
D own there was something strange
D own there was something curious
E ven though there's a light, I am still scared
N ow I'm down there, I'm shaking with fear

T he mysterious something
R ests still there
E verything was quiet
A fter I took a step closer
S ure, I was frightened
U nder the floorboards
R ests still that something
E ven though it's still there
S urely I was never to go there again.

Jessica Herron (10)
Upton Junior School

AN UNKNOWN PATIENT

An unknown patient you will remain
A man of mystery, with no name
Follow a rainbow, not a star
It will guide you to who you are

Without a hope, or so it seems
He vaguely remembers in his dreams
A riddle he once overheard
Harder to catch than a bird!

Then suddenly in the room appeared
A rainbow, which might sound weird
And above that striped and coloured dress
Smiled a face so young and fresh!

A girl who left and caused such pain
That he was left without a name
Now in this child, she had come back
With the sudden thought, his name was Jack!

Lara Maley (11)
Upton Junior School

HIDDEN TREASURES

H idden treasures,
I n the deep,
D iving, swooping under the seas,
D rifting close,
E verywhere to see,
N ot a sound.

T o the ground as we went deeper,
R eaching out to coral near the shark,
E xcited to see,
A s we opened the box,
S lowly, slowly,
U nder the sea, he
R emembered the locks,
E ntering the box,
S lowly, slowly.

David Armstrong (10)
Upton Junior School

MILO

In the attic, above my room
Lays something precious of mine, not a watch,
Not a gift, but a photo,
A photo which has been with me since I took it
And now I remember when I got him.
I remember by looking at it.
It's a picture of my dog - a Jack Russell.
I got him a few days after he was born.
He lit up my whole life.
Every day after school I knew I had someone there for me,
My dog and now there is nothing.
In my house there is nothing now,
Because he's flying with angels.
My treasure,
My memory,
Milo.

Liam McCabe (10)
Upton Junior School

HIDDEN TREASURES

T   reasure is anywhere if you look hard enough,
R   ed, green, blue, any colour is treasure,
E   verything is treasure, your dog, cat, even a book that you love,
A   treasure is honey from a hive, a dog's bone and jewels,
S   eeing brothers, cousins, is real treasure,
U   nderwater cities to be rediscovered,
R   eal treasure is a newborn baby,
E   veryone has a treasure, if you look and see.

Jack Greenslade (10)
Upton Junior School

Hidden Treasures

H idden treasures, where do you find them?
I would look down on the beach
D ig, dig, dig a hole so very . . .
D eep. I found something, it could be
E arrings, but no, hang on - I think it's a
N ecklace. I wouldn't want it to be a

T ea bag because it would be all soggy.
R ing that would be worth some money.
E verybody's walking by and kicking sand
A nd what are you doing? They're filling up my hole,
S top it now, run away but mind the
U mbrella shading me from the sun. Don't want you to fall.
R ing? Please let it be a ring. An
E merald would be nice - oh I found it,
S eaweed, stupid, slimy seaweed.

Amie Borg (10)
Upton Junior School

Golden Coins

G littering coins in a cave,
O ut of sight in a grave,
L ook out, look out, wandering soul,
D own below, in the hole,
E agerly looking after its stash,
N ever leaving the shimmering cash.

C ome on in, if you dare,
O ut of that cold sea air,
I nto the dark, gloomy light,
N ever leave, you'll die of fright,
S hining, glittering, golden coins.

Danny Agar (11)
Upton Junior School

HIDDEN TREASURES

Hidden under your feet right now,
Is something shiny in the ground,
Down, down, down really deep,
Is something valuable you might meet.

Is it gold or is it silver?
No one knows what it can be,
A diamond ring, a gold watch,
I'm sure there's something under that tree.

Hidden under the deep blue sea,
Is something shiny in the sand,
Deeper and deeper, really deep,
I'm sure it's hiding under that reef.

Is it gold or is it silver?
No one knows what it can be,
A diamond ring, a gold watch,
I'm sure there's something under the sea.

Hidden up in the darkest nights,
Is something shiny in the clouds,
It's not gold and it's not silver,
But it is the love that goes around.

I don't mind that it's not gold or silver,
I don't mind that it's not something I can see,
Who needs a diamond ring or a gold watch,
Love all around is for me.

Tiffany Atwill (11)
Upton Junior School

ALL ON A MIDSUMMER'S NIGHT

The moon shone through the dark, dark night
The air was still, the stars twinkled by
Then through the open window came a wisp of hair and then a head
The body came soon after, as did the feet
'Come find the hidden treasure,' he now quietly said
(All on a midsummer's night)

'What treasure?' I exclaimed out loud
There is no treasure here, I thought
'Here is only sadness - my family is poor'
The wink of his eye said don't be afraid
'The treasure I seek is something more,'
(All on a midsummer's night)

'The treasure I talk of is as sweet as honey
It sings out loud like a bird in the treetops
This treasure is called happiness - of which I give to you,'
'But how and where can I find it?' I cried
The stranger smiled and took my hand, his other - he laid on my heart
(All on a midsummer's night)

'Right there, my dear,' said he
'Hidden from sight, the treasure's buried here
Not an X but a heart to mark the spot
Where you will find true happiness
For your family, true happiness, forever and ever.'
(All on a midsummer's night)

Then suddenly, gone was the stranger
Vanished, completely from sight
So dark was the sky that night
Though the moon and stars shone bright
All on this midsummer's night
What a perfect midsummer's night.

Alicia Wright (11)
Upton Junior School

SHOULD WE OR NOT?

H is treasure was hidden under the floor
I t was very valuable
D ad didn't know that Mum and I had it
D an, our dog, sniffed it out
E veryone was poor in our family
N ow why can't we sell the valuable jewels?

T o tell Dad would be very hard
R ings, there were emeralds, sapphires and diamonds
E arrings, only a few pairs with gems on them
A nd even eight necklaces
S adly Mum said I had to tell Dad
U sually I would tell anything to Dad
R eally this was too hard for me
E ven telling my brother was hard
S o do you think we sold some or not?

Chloe Lloyd (10)
Upton Junior School

A GARDEN'S TREASURE

Think of a garden's tall long grass,
Where children sing and play and dance,
Squirrels and birds all make their nests,
They all do try their very best.
When winter comes, the animals freeze,
Throughout the forest are bare trees,
When winter leaves, the spring returns,
The dandelions all sway and turn.
The summer heat means time for a tan,
When sitting down with a drink in a can.

Daniel Jackson (10)
Upton Junior School

TREASURE HUNT

Oh, to find a treasure chest,
You must hurry to beat the rest!
Follow the map and you will see,
Where the hidden gold will be.

A cross will show you,
The place you're going to.
Over mountains, down streams,
Until you come to the place of your dreams.

You'll have to dig down deep,
There'll be no time to sleep.
Soon the treasure chest will appear,
But have the pirates beaten you there?

Tim Cottis (11)
Upton Junior School

THE STONY PATH

As I walk along this stony path
I see a shiny penny
And as I turn around to look,
I realise there are many.

As I walk along this stony path
I see a glistening spoon,
It suddenly reminds me of
The brightly shining moon.

As I've walked along this stony path
I realised from the start,
The hidden treasures are inside me,
Deep within my heart.

Katie Jolly (11)
Upton Junior School

Golden Trophy

H idden under the ground,
I dug it up, I did not know about it.
D id anybody know it was down there?
D on't take it to a museum - it's mine.
E ager was I to see what it was.
N eighbourhood wanted to see the golden trophy.

T able it stood on for neighbourhood to see.
R eally wanted Gran to get out of bed to see the golden trophy.
E arly that morning they crowded to see.
A buse it some people did.
S ure, it was the best thing in the world.
U nusual it was to see.
R eally beautiful it was to see.
E veryone, do you think it is the most beautiful treasure?

Aaron Palmer (11)
Upton Junior School

My Treasures

My treasure is not
Silver or gold
It is a lovely dog
And a puppy you can hold

They are very good
Can do sit and paw
If you ever met them
You would want to see them more

Like caramel and chocolate
They are blonde and brown
They walk around
As if they wear the crown

But the best thing
Is they belong to me
I love them loads
As you can probably see.

Rachel Murphy (10)
Upton Junior School

Hidden Treasures

H idden in the attic, under the floor,
I s it treasure? Well, no one can see it.
D amaged, tattered, broken.
D own the drain, into a puddle
E ven precious gold - like necklaces, rings and coins.
N ever open it, it will be very hard.

T ight to pull - throw it in the sea.
R est in peace so no one can disturb it.
E erie and mucky - don't touch it.
A te by bugs - night and day.
S ee it being carried by a dog.
U se a crowbar to open it.
R elease it - it is gone.
E ast it has travelled.
S ure, you are happy - hidden treasure.

Liam Packer (11)
Upton Junior School

TREASURES OF MY MIND

H idden at the bottom of the sea
I nside a shipwrecked boat
D own, lying on the seabed
D ead and gone forever
E nchanted, lost or cursed
N ever losing power

T ruly magnificent
R eturned from ever resting
E mber burning bright
A t the core of a volcano
S izzling hot rock
U nbearable heat
R ippling lava
E pic journeys
S leeping deep.

Rebekah Campbell (11)
Upton Junior School

MAGPIE

As I swoop and soar across the sky,
I feel the breezy air against my feathery chest,
Suddenly I notice something I like best.

As I hover to check the coast is clear,
I notice something that I fear,
A cunning fox, who is very near.

I flee back to my nest,
With my injured wing,
To try and get some rest.

Georgina Ann Turner (11)
Upton Junior School

Hundred Pounds

H undred pounds are the best.
U nderneath my pillow, I wish.
N ice people only have £100,
D own on the ground, I see money.
R un and get the money!
E xcept the children.
D own on the ground I see even more money.

P ocket money is the best.
O utside, people throwing money around and around,
U nder my feet, just money and even more money.
N o more money on the floor!
D oh, the money's all gone,
S o you can see, I like money!

James Fleischer (11)
Upton Junior School

The Wreckage

As I climbed upon the stone,
I realised I was alone,
Searching high and searching low,
I come across a sparkling glow.

Underneath my soggy sock,
I realised it was a shiny rock,
As I reached out with my hand,
I just looked back on the land.

I was starting to feel tense,
Beginning to shake, I could sense,
I think it's treasure, it's shining bright,
I can't believe my eyes, I shout with delight.

Melissa Jones (11)
Upton Junior School

HIDDEN TREASURES

H idden in the sky so high
I nside a bird body
D ead, dead, dead he is
D ead and gone to Heaven
E nded his life forever
N ever coming back to Earth

T he treasure is an ace of spades
R est at the bottom of the pack
E veryone could play with him
A ce of spades could take you anywhere
S un is so low to him
U nder the clouds, so high
R est in the sky
E veryone could play with him
S o if you see a pack of cards with an ace of spades at the bottom of the pack, say hello for me.

Samuel Ball (10)
Upton Junior School

HIDDEN TREASURE

The question that I long to ask
What is the treasure in that flask?
Is it gold, fine enough to drink?
Is it a key, does it link?
I'd better try and find it fast.

Can I find it now?
Yes, but how?
Under the sea, is it there,
Or maybe in a fox's lair?
Let's not have a row.

We will find that treasure,
Maybe it's in a chest of leather?
Digging down very deep,
Mound upon mound, in a heap,
Will we find that treasure, ever?

Gemma West (10)
Upton Junior School

TREASURES

A treasure can be anything,
anything you want.
It could be a magic ring
or a frog that can sing.
It could be a tree that follows you around
or a fish that can live underground.
It could be a book with magic powers
or a castle with fifty towers.
It could be a flower that can talk
or a house that can walk.
It could be a super, new, magic shower
or a piece of bubblegum that changes colour every hour.
It could be a bird that can dance
or a pen that can prance.
It could be a pudding that comes alive
or a gnome that can dive.
It could be an ant that grows big
or a butterfly that wears a wig.
A treasure can be anything,
anything you want.

Joanne Hodd (10)
Upton Junior School

HIDDEN TREASURE

H igh on a hill
I n a sunken boat
D eep in a vast ocean
D igging for treasure
E arth to be moved
N othing to say, it's not metal

T humb through pages of an old book
R eading can be a treasure
E njoying the opening of a flower bud
A rrival of spring
S eeing the mountains
U p high in the sky
R eaching to the stars
E njoy your journey to find your treasure
   It can be anything you want it to be.

Victoria Gladden (11)
Upton Junior School

TREASURE

Treasure is everyone's dream,
But treasure can be anything,
What is treasure?
It's not just your pleasure,
Treasure is your family and your love,
You're like a pair of two white doves.

Leigh Marie Evans (10)
Upton Junior School

HIDDEN TREASURE

H idden at the bottom of the sea
I n a desert island
D eep beneath the dusty sand
D eep beneath the salty sea
E nter the mystery world
N o one must know about this place

T ake a look around the island
R ushing for the mystic treasure
E ating some fruits for energy
A nger strikes your little face
S earching for the map
U nderground mining
R eaching for shelter
E nchantments found along the way.

Jade Holloway (10)
Upton Junior School

TREASURE WITHIN

A treasure within a smile,
Measures up to a mile,
Far and wide, the room's alight,
It makes the room so bright.

A treasure within a tear,
Can last a long year,
Crying is not just sadness,
Sometimes relief or gladness.

The main treasures are hiding in yourself,
The mind, body and soul,
Family and friends are the treasures that make you, you.

Jade Mary Starmer (10)
Upton Junior School

HIDDEN TREASURES

H idden treasure,
I s it still around?
D id it ever exist?
D o you believe in it?
E nded, has it ended?
N o one knows.

T reasure, treasure
R ealistic or not?
E xhausted yet?
A ll stop,
S urely it can't be true or can it?
U ntil someone finds it,
R eaching, pulling, finding what you can,
E veryone is looking for one thing,
S omeone in the end might find it.

Kate Sanders (11)
Upton Junior School

WHAT IS A TREASURE?

What is a treasure?
Is it enjoyable, like leisure?
Is it something precious, like my dog?
Is it ugly, like a frog?
What is a treasure?

What is a treasure?
Is it pleasure?
Is it my mum and dad?
Is it something sad?
What is a treasure?

Claire Orchard (10)
Upton Junior School

HIDDEN TREASURES

H idden treasures beneath the ground
I ntelligence is needed to find it
D ig down, dig deep
D on't stop now
E nergy is lost and coming in
N eeding help, you won't find it now!

T hese things aren't really true, they
R ead it in books and find all these facts
E xisting, no it isn't!
A ll it is, is a feeling
S ticking in your brain
U nder people, look and see
R ealising there's no treasure there
E nding their search yet again
S earches will never end.

Claire Stokes (11)
Upton Junior School

MY DREAM CAME TRUE

Soaring, soaring across the sky,
Swooping, gliding low and high,
In between the clouds and the air,
Is some treasure lying there?

I'm looking through the long, tall grass,
Hoping that it's gold or brass,
Silver or bronze, it will not be,
But to my surprise, it's the deep blue sea.

Laura Stockley (11)
Upton Junior School

DEMONS' TREASURE

D eadly demons walk the Earth.
E ating food and people.
M ore and more they grow.
O verwhelmed with fright.
N ever, ever resting.
S oaring around the world.

H aving all they want.
A lways destroying something.
V ery powerful and strong.
E veryone being destroyed.

A ll own special names.

H ouses turning from brick to rubble.
E ntering the danger zone.
A monster eating every bone.
R ipping walls of buildings down.
T he treasure to be found, the heart of the demon.

Travers Gardner (10)
Upton Junior School

HIDDEN TREASURE

Hidden treasures are here all the time,
Some of them are inside me,
Some are in the sun and moon
And some under the sea.

Hidden treasures are here all the time,
Could even be a broken dart,
Diamonds and gold and silver too,
Inside me is my heart.

Hidden treasures are here all the time,
We don't know where they are,
One thing I know for certain,
They don't always come from lands afar.

Claire Thomson (11)
Upton Junior School

MY TREASURE

I was eight-years-old
Searching my world
Wondering where I should go
Should I go upstairs
Or in the loft?
Should I go see the magic show?

I scrambled upstairs
Into my mum's room
And suddenly I was in a tomb
Photos of my family
Were hanging around
A photo of me, lay on the ground

Next to my photo
There was a golden box
On which there was a painting of a fox
Inside the box, to my surprise
There was a picture of me
And my nan inside

I said to myself, I'll keep this box
And the picture
Until I die
And forever.

Lara Hackney (10)
Upton Junior School

HIDDEN TREASURES

A is for the alligators that cross the quiet stream,
B is for the beaming sun that brings the magic into our world,
C is for the clumsy clowns that make the children laugh,
D is for the daring life that lives inside our hearts,
E is for the enchantment that God brings in us each day,
F is for the frightened deer that runs along the field,
G is for the giant tower that lives unknown for now,
H is for the happy humans that live their life today,
I is for the intelligence that lies inside our brains,
J is for the joking that grows towards the world,
K is for the kettle that boils inside the kitchen,
L is for the looking-glass that Alice crosses scarcely,
M is for the many creatures that live under the sea,
N is for the naughty children who are rude, selfish and mean,
O is for the cute otters that swim about in water,
P is for the parents who love you very much,
Q is for the Queen that looks after our world,
R is for the racing hearts that lie scared and alone,
S is for the stern people that pay for what they do,
T is for the golden treasure that lies at the end of the rainbow,
U is the unicorns that live in fairy tales,
V is for the Victorians that children study now,
W is for the famous William Shakespeare whose poems are excellent,
X is for the x-rays that injured people have,
Y is for the yachts and boats that travel the coast,
Z is for the zebras that scurry down the hill!

Rachel Hewitt (10)
Upton Junior School

HIDDEN TREASURES

Hidden treasures could be . . .

A ny form of gold or silver
B alls that could bounce as high as the stars
C locks that take you forward in time
D inosaurs that are as small and fluffy as dogs
E ggs that would tell your fortune when you crack them
F rogs whose eyes are made of chocolate
G enies that could help you with your maths
H ippos that can take you under the sea
I gloos that won't melt in the sun
J elly with gold coins in the middle
K ites that can fly you to the moon
L emurs that live in the cupboard and tidy your room at night
M oney that grows on trees
N its that wash your hair for you
O ranges with sweets instead of pips
P ocket-sized pies
Q uiet after a busy day
R oofs that fold out into a swimming pool
S nakes that protect you from harm
T offees that last forever
U mbrellas that appear when it is raining
V ery good friends
W indows that show you all the good things in your future
X -ray eyes! (Hee, hee)
Y ummy things in my lunch box
Z zzzz at the end of a hard day.

Robin Peacock (11)
Upton Junior School

HIDDEN TREASURES

H igh above the cloudy sky live the treasures
I ndigo, gold, silver too
D angerous, kind or just shy
D eadly, poisonous or blue
E nchanting, so give us a clue
N ever-ending treasure

T reassure of all kinds
R each and find
E ncyclopedia and time
A pple of gold
S ticks of silver
U nattended secrets to be found
R eigning kings of gold
E verlasting in the cloudy sky
S ecrets to be unfolded.

Hannah Bolt (10)
Upton Junior School

HIDDEN TREASURES

Hidden treasures,
Lost, untold,
Many search very bold,
Then they too are lost, untold,
Still the treasure's lost in the cold.

Hidden, sunk, lost too,
Who will find it? Maybe you.
In the shipwreck, lost, untold,
Venture out in the cold.

Killion McKenzie (10)
Upton Junior School

FIFTY POUND NOTES

F   ifty pound notes are the best
I   n every shop there's something you want
F   lying toys like boomerangs and kites
T   he ultimate toy is a pogo stick
Y   elling and screaming, going so high

P   ounding and prancing through the sky
O   nwards and upwards the pogo stick goes
U   nder and over, through I go
N   ear and far in the street
D   own the dark alley, I lose my balance

N   ow I'm buying a remote control car
O   ver the drain it jumps by far
T   aking a risk over an open manhole
E   verything trampled on but not this car
S   lipping and sliding on the ice

A   nd now I'm buying a trampoline
R   eally high I'm bouncing
E   ven though bouncing makes me hot and sweaty

T   rampolining is so much fun
H   ow about practising in the sun
E   ntering a trampolining competition

B   et I can do some premier bouncing
E   very minute in the air
S   uddenly I see a glinting object
T   ry to get it but I can't quite reach.

Ryan Birch (10)
Upton Junior School

PHARAOH'S TREASURE

H idden treasure we shall find,
I n the darkness of the night,
D own in the jungle it shall be,
D own with all the killer bees,
E nter the clearing in the centre,
N ow one more step and we're in danger.

T reading softly on the leaves,
R eally close are the killer bees,
E nter the tomb with the treasure,
A pharaoh lying there with pleasure,
S hall we die in the tomb?
U ttering, 'No! Blow up the tomb with a boom!'
R unning fast, we grab the chest,
E vening falls, now to rest.

Dylan Smith (10)
Upton Junior School